TALES FROM THE
GONZAGA BULLDOGS
LOCKER ROOM

TALES FROM THE
GONZAGA BULLDOGS
LOCKER ROOM

A COLLECTION OF THE GREATEST
BULLDOG STORIES EVER TOLD

DAVE BOLING

FOREWORD BY
MARK FEW

SPORTS
PUBLISHING

*Countless contributors—seen and unseen,
famous and obscure, embraced or estranged—helped
elevate Gonzaga University basketball to a level of
national prominence. This book is dedicated to their efforts.*

Contents

Foreword

First of all, I have to say how blessed I've been to be able to work with the players who have come through the Gonzaga basketball program. I think one thing that separates Gonzaga from a lot of programs out there is that in so many ways it's a family. Once you're in the family, you're in it for life. The best part of the job—better than the NCAA Tournament wins and the championships—is building the relationships with the players through the years. We go from being coaches and players to being lifelong friends once they've finished playing. It's so rewarding to see how successful they are, as attorneys and engineers and teachers. Probably even greater than that is seeing the wonderful parents that they've become. I don't know how many other programs really have such a "family" feel to them.

The administration and the university foster that kind of relationship; that's Gonzaga, once you go there, you're a part of it for life. For whatever reason, people always seem to want to come back and keep in touch with the people they met here. That's probably even more so with our basketball program; the character of the kids is such that they seem to want to hang on to the experience by staying close with friends and keeping in touch. That's really the essence of it.

Over the years we've had some very strong individual personalities and characters. Everybody is different, and we welcome and encourage that. They may be as different as a gregarious and outgoing Frenchman with long dreadlocks to a quiet, competitive guy from Walla Walla who hardly talks at all. But they all have a common denominator; they all share the same quality: They are willing to put themselves aside and put the good of the team first. It's probably the mix of these personalities that makes it so enjoyable. You see an Anthony Reason from Ocala, Florida, and Compton (California) Community College running around with Blake Stepp and Dan Dickau from the Pacific Northwest. They love him and he loves them. They enjoy sharing each other's culture, and the mixture of personalities works so well because they also share those common goals.

When you put all those ingredients together, and you end up finding talented guys with diverse backgrounds who want to come together and put the team first, you almost can't help but be successful. Because of all that, you just have a heck of a lot of fun coaching those types of guys, and you truly enjoy being around them. The icing on the cake is that we've been so successful, which makes it a win-win-win situation for all of us.

A part of the program's success, too, has been our ability to keep the same staff together. That just doesn't happen in college basketball. As a staff, we've always had a very, very high quality of life here, and now we make sure we take the extra time to put family first. It helps so much to have a staff that's been together forever and understands what it takes and has a feel for how players will fit in as a part of the team. Then you have a guy like trainer Steve DeLong, who almost nobody knows about from the outside, but who has been as valuable a staff member as anyone. He keeps coaches in line, toughens the players up, and is the players' friend. He IS Gonzaga.

If I had to pick one example that shows what this program is all about, I'd point to the last game in "The Kennel" in the spring of 2004. We had over 100 former players back for the game … spanning generations. Their willingness to do that is remarkable. The fun they had and the genuineness of their emotions … that shows what this has been all about. You see the same thing when you go to a wedding of one of the players; you'll see not only his teammates but guys from the generations before him and after him. It's impressive; they all grew to be friends because they're Gonzaga basketball players. It sounds corny, but that kind of thing is not commonplace in college basketball.

I hope that *Tales from the Gonzaga Hardwood* helps fans see these players as the great people they are. Lost in all the wins and the NCAA appearances is the fact that a guy like Ronny Turiaf has probably made 100 charity visits in his time here. Or a guy like Brian Michaelson, who a lot of fans haven't heard of, has been doing that sort of thing all along because he wears a Gonzaga jersey. Or the guys reading stories to first grade classes in town. What you'll read about in this book is not just Casey Calvary making a big tip-in or Richie Frahm stroking a three, or Dan Dickau making great passes, it's the blood, sweat and tears, literally, that went into this program.

I'd like to personally thank each and every player who has come through this program for making it such an awesome experience in my life, and in the lives of our staff. It's been a true blessing to be able to work with them and continue to have great relationships with them after they've finished playing. Thank you.

—Mark Few, November 2004

Acknowledgments

Coach Mark Few likes to call Gonzaga University "a people place." That is meant to describe the helpful, accommodating and caring attitude that pervades the campus. That was certainly the case during the preparation of this book. Athletic director Mike Roth and coaches Few, Bill Grier, Leon Rice, Tommy Lloyd and Jerry Krause all generously scanned their memory caches for the best recollections from over the years, as did former coach Dan Monson, now at the University of Minnesota. Sports information director Oliver Pierce must be thanked for his assistance, guidance and archival memory. Trainer Steve DeLong and former baseball coach Steve Hertz, longtime GU fixtures, graciously shared their insights. The late Father Tony Lehmann, a man of pure spirit, contributed a legacy of wisdom and patience and kindness still felt strongly around Gonzaga even years after his passing. Former coach and athletic director Dan Fitzgerald is appreciated for being a font of colorful quotes and memorable moments during his Gonzaga tenure. And mostly a debt of gratitude is owed to the Zags for being multidimensional individuals with compelling experiences. They provided a rich, broad mixture of both relevance and irreverence. After all, being helpful is commendable, but being interesting ... that's the real treasure. Thanks go to them for being so willing to share with me their tales.

Introduction

Over by the library, a statue of Bing Crosby stands in perpetual nonchalance, barely more inert than the low-key crooner seemed in life. For decades, this most famous son of Gonzaga University appropriately represented the essence of the drowsy little Jesuit school in a leafy neighborhood on the north bank of the Spokane River.

These days, the spirit of the school would be better captured by a sculpture of Dan Dickau pulling up for a three-point shot, or Matt Santangelo frozen in mid-drive down the lane, or Casey Calvary hanging from some rim after a seismic dunk. And, of course, a carved-in-stone likeness of John Stockton would be required, marble eyes scanning the floor, with the ball ready to be distributed through an opening only he could detect.

This is the contemporary Gonzaga, a place that has rocketed across an improbable trajectory from basketball backwater, to home for a cuddly little gang of March overachievers, to the fevered residence of a team that annually visits the upper reaches of the national polls. And while a generation of basketball fans around the country may now recite GU's NCAA Tournament record, many might need to ask, "Bing Who?"

Gonzaga's caste-busting ascension disrupted college basketball's entrenched pecking order. Unrecognized entities emerge every spring for a round or two before the forces of competitive gravity drag them back down to their normal niche. But for the Zags this has not been a singular surfacing. In the span of six seasons, 1999 through 2004, the Zags averaged more than 26 wins and made consecutive NCAA appearances, completing what appears to be a repeatable, sustainable—and apparently permanent—relocation to the top of the national hoops heap.

Gonzaga's transmutation into a national powerhouse from under-funded also-ran, relying on pluck and feisty underdoggery, required a convergence of factors. There's been a continuum of coaches serving apprenticeships through the ranks. Along the way, they've adapted and refined and improved the product. But they've mostly adhered to a core mission of conscripting tough kids with consuming dedication, guys who understand the game and the nearly extinct concept of success through selflessness and unity.

The talent level has surged, but Gonzaga is still a place where a walk-on from Walla Walla, like guard Kyle Bankhead, could start on the No. 2-ranked team in the nation. One recent survey of NCAA basketball players showed Gonzaga's incoming freshmen to have the second highest grade-point averages in the nation (3.38), trailing only Stanford. Yet it remains a program where the coach will evict the players from their cozy locker room if they leave it a mess.

Named after St. Aloysius Gonzaga, the Patron Saint of Youth, Gonzaga started out as a frontier boarding school for boys in 1887. Spokane, a railroad town built around the mining, lumber and farming economy of the region, was leveled by fire in 1889, but Gonzaga, on the north side of the river, was spared.

As for athletics, Gonzaga was an early regional football power. Although the school gave up the game around World War II, Gonzaga has as many graduates in the Pro Football Hall of Fame (Ray Flaherty and Tony Canadeo) as in-state football powers Washington and Washington State. Gus Dorais, Knute Rockne's teammate at Notre Dame and among the first accomplished practitioners of the forward pass, was Gonzaga's first full-time football coach. The best of the early Gonzaga football players, however, may have been triple-threat back and linebacker Houston Stockton, whose grandson, John, would play a little basketball at GU and in the NBA.

Gonzaga came late to Division I basketball, not elevating to that level until 1958. One notable early achievement came in 1961 when Frank Burgess, now a federal district judge in Tacoma, led the Zags, and the nation, in scoring with a 32.4-point average.

Coach/athletic director Dan Fitzgerald midwifed the early stages of the modern emergence of GU basketball, leading a change in conferences from the Big Sky to the West Coast in 1979. Outside the Pacific Northwest, though, Gonzaga remained anonymous. And if not entirely unknown in the region, it was still frequently mispronounced, as PA announcers at games loved to say "Gon-ZAWG-a," not "Gon-ZAG-a." Even worse, at times, the team was said to represent: "Gonzales University."

Fitzgerald, proud of his Irish heritage and rugged upbringing in San Francisco, constructed teams that were reflections of himself ... tough, fearless, and determined to outwork and outprepare opponents. Players were taught to make the extra pass, take the charge, and beat each other bloody every day in practice. For a time, many tended to party with much the same collegial vigor afterward, but took pride in still being able to make it to class and graduate with distinction.

Fitzgerald forever altered the course of the program by signing an undersized but hypercompetitive point guard from the neighborhood in 1980. John Stockton engendered little recruiting interest coming out of Gonzaga Prep, but given his family history and proximity, he seemed predestined to go to Gonzaga U, anyway. But even the willful Stockton couldn't lift Gonzaga into the postseason.

Although Fitzgerald later resigned as athletic director during an investigation for misappropriation of funds, he shaped a framework for the program, and almost assured its continued success by hiring a trio of young assistants—Dan Monson, Mark Few and Bill Grier. None ever played Division I basketball, but they shared a vision of where GU basketball could be headed. More importantly, they generated the energy and drive to get it there.

As the program earned regional esteem for the grit and the grades of its players, Fitzgerald's teams nonetheless enjoyed little more than middling success through the 1980s. It reached the nadir in the 1989-90 season, when the team finished 8-20, but a group of talented redshirts sat out that season in preparation for GU's first real run at basketball repute.

Within two years, that group won 20 for the first time since the school arrived at the Division I level, and two years after that, a 22-win season and WCC regular-season title led to GU's first postseason invitation. The first substantive proof of sustainable excellence emerged with 21 wins in 1994. That year, Fitzgerald and his staff roused the team to a conference tournament title—after a league start of 0-6—and received the automatic NCAA bid that accompanies it.

Fitzgerald tacked on another NIT appearance in 1996 before abdicating his post to make way for Dan Monson. The son of veteran Oregon and Idaho basketball coach Don Monson, Dan Monson took over in 1997 as Fitzgerald focused solely on his athletic director's duties. Monson immediately notified college basketball observers of Gonzaga's upwardly mobile intent by winning the Top of the World Classic in Fairbanks, Alaska, with consecutive upset wins over Tulsa, Mississippi State and No. 5-ranked Clemson.

But given the Zags' skimpy portfolio, 24 wins and the WCC regular-season title weren't attractive enough to land an at-large NCAA Tournament invitation that season, and the Zags, formerly delighted with any postseason attention, suddenly found themselves unsatisfied with another NIT berth.

A hefty 28 wins in 1999 earned the unheralded Zags nothing more than a 12th seed into the West Regionals at Seattle's Key Arena. But in front of a hugely partisan gathering, they responded with a 12-point win over fifth-seeded Minnesota. And in the first truly legitimizing victory, the Zags—suddenly proclaimed Cinderellas on a national level—then handed No. 2-seed Stanford a 12-point defeat.

Florida then fell by a point to the Zags in the Sweet 16 as Casey Calvary tipped in the winning basket with four seconds remaining, leaving GU to face Connecticut for the West Regional title ... 40 minutes away from the Final Four. Gonzaga trailed the eventual national champion Huskies by just a point with a minute remaining before falling 67-62.

The exposure gave the Zags permanent recognition in bracket lore, and landed Monson a huge raise from the University of Minnesota. After lengthy internal debate, Monson accepted the job of coaching the scandal-plagued Golden Gophers, and Few moved over a seat to lead the Zags into the 1999-2000 season.

Improbably, Few tacked on five more consecutive NCAA Tournament trips. When coaching vacancies at national powerhouse universities arise, Few's name is immediately tossed into the list of top candidates. Big-money offers haven't lured Few from Gonzaga, though. And the school, riding upon the surging basketball prestige, no longer suffers confusion with some mythical "Gonzales University." The fiscal effects? Freshman enrollment more than doubled during that span, from in the 400 range to something in the 900 range. "The Kennel" was suddenly too small to hold overflow crowds, and a new, $25 million, 6,000-seat arena was set to open for the 2004 season.

Now around NCAA Tournament time every March, Bing's statue is enlivened by t-shirts that read, "Go Zags," and imply his posthumous approval of his old school's new image.

Although it's no longer the anonymous little university that no one could correctly pronounce, Gonzaga's basketball program still has its quirks. There's still the characters, although fewer dedicated partiers than seemed the case with earlier crews. One Zag or another is still sequestered in the gym, polishing his game on a 24-hour basis, much as Stockton did a generation earlier. And Stockton, who still lives a few blocks away, sneaks in to play ratball with the contemporary Zags, making his legacy one that is both tangible and immediate.

This introduction with skeletal facts was required because we're adhering to no rigid structure in the body of this book; nothing chronological, linear or extensively biographical. This is not intended to supply a thorough historical narrative nor analyze the evolution of this basketball program. It doesn't try to mention all the key characters; it won't go back through the early days of coaches like Hank Anderson and Adrian Buoncristiani, and their players—although those could fill many chapters.

This is more about the stories than the stars, so there will be more mention of a colorful role player like Mark Spink than there will be of, say, a focused and gifted standout such as Matt Santangelo.

It won't examine the probation resulting from Dan Fitzgerald's directorship, which, the NCAA stressed, was not the sort of behavior designed to give Gonzaga a competitive edge. Why? Because it's boring as flat beer. Fitzgerald, a walking archive of many of the best stories, declined to contribute new material to the project. His comments in this book are from earlier interviews and player recollections.

We have assiduously sought to avoid stats in favor of quips, dreary controversy in favor of wisecracks, and wanted to give the practical jokes equal standing to the game-winning strategies. In short, the goal is to present the Zags as multidimensional entities rather than merely uniformed athletes.

Really, it's a collection of the best stories and tidbits meant to entertain and take the reader behind the scenes, into the huddle and the locker room. This, then, is a compendium of "tales," as the title promises. If we did it right, the reader should feel as if he's been invited to pull up a bar stool at Jack and Dan's and sit in on a "virtual" reunion of Zags throughout the recent era, to hear their best stories, to share their laughs, and to feel what the Gonzaga experience was really like for them.

CHAPTER ONE

Four Cornerstone Moments

Leap of Faith

To the Gonzaga University coaching staff, it may have seemed like a sucker bet. At the start of the 1991-92 season, a cocky corps of Zag players envisioned a breakthrough, 20-win season and offered to put a little wager on it to add interest. The Zags had never exceeded that win total as a Division I school, and it had been just two years since they bottomed out at 8-20, so the coaches probably would have agreed to just about any proposed pay off.

"We made them promise if we won 20 that they'd go to a bridge over the Spokane River and jump in," point guard Geoff Goss said. Head coach Dan Fitzgerald was exempt from the challenge.

"We didn't even try to get Fitz in on it," Goss said. "Because he'd have said, 'Get out of my face, I'm your head coach.'"

But assistants Dan Monson, Mark Few and Bill Grier were included, as was veteran coach Jerry Krause. Monson, Few and Grier were still at reasonable bridge-jumping ages, but the widely respected and scholarly Krause, who has a doctorate degree and is the author of more than two dozen books, could have been excused for trying to wiggle out of the foolhardy pact. After all, he graduated from college in 1959, before the other assistants had been born.

Perhaps motivated by the image of their coaches' synchronized dive, the Zags beat San Diego and Santa Clara in the West Coast Conference Tournament to reach the 20 wins before losing by three to Portland in the title game.

To hit the magic 20 number represented a symbolic leap for the Zags, a transition, a bridge between eras. The core of the team was sophomores, and conference contention would be assured for at least several seasons.

So the coaches gathered at the river to reward their players' excellence by performing an act of stupidity.

It was April, and the Spokane River as it rushes past Gonzaga at a time of surging snowmelt runoff is treacherous and icy. But stripped to their skivvies, holding hands like paper dolls, they flew off the bridge. Including Krause.

"That was like watching Einstein jump off the bridge," Goss said of Krause's plunge. "We were all pretty impressed that they lived up to their part of the deal. For them to do that was unbelievable to us."

Center Jeff Brown, who had engineered the wager, grew genuinely worried about the potential danger.

"The river was really flowing and that water was not warm," Brown said. "There was honestly a part of me worrying that Coach Krause's ticker would stop when he hit that water. I mean, here's Few and Mons and Billy, all in their early 30s. But it's like a 20- or 25-foot drop off the Centennial Bridge."

Didn't the young coaches try to talk Krause out of it, to make some excuses to save him the danger and indignity?

"Heck no, misery loves company," Monson said. "Besides, he was in better shape than me even if he was 100 years old."

"Yes, let's say I was more mature," Krause said of his vintage at the time. "Let's just say I was into my 50s."

And the feel of hitting the water? "Like jumping into an ice cube," Krause said.

Regrets about making such a perilous bet?

"Nah," Krause said. "It was fun."

Fun, once everybody scrambled to shore. This event amused the players and certainly revealed the staff's willingness to take just about any risk that might lead to competitive advancement.

But there's considerable relief among those involved that acts of daring are no longer required as inducements to get the Zags their 20-win seasons, because they're swimming in much deeper water these days.

Hiring the Three Amigos

Gonzaga was named after Jesuit Saint Aloysius Gonzaga, the Patron Saint of Youth. If there were a similar designation for coaches, Dan Fitzgerald might be considered for canonization. In stages over the late 1980s and early 1990s, Fitzgerald hired three young assistants with little or no college coaching experience. None had even played the game in Division I.

He worked them hard and he gave them verbal prodding, but he also gave them all chances they probably wouldn't have gotten from another Division I head coach. And as Dan Monson and Mark Few have succeeded him, and Bill Grier has moved up incrementally, they have expanded and improved on the Fitzgerald product.

"Opportunity," Few said when asked of the prime gift of Fitzgerald. "He gave us all a chance. And he let us coach; he delegated. He basically turned recruiting over to us. He taught us how to evaluate, which was huge."

Fitzgerald's obsession with preparedness lodged permanently in the minds of the young assistants, too.

"At first, early on, it was our fear of not being prepared that drove us," Few said. "If we weren't ready and he found out, he'd throw a fit. If they ran a play we didn't have, we'd hear about it. But then we did it because it was important for us to convince the players that we were going to be better prepared than whatever team we were playing."

At times, GU players would hear a play called, and they'd tell the man they were guarding where he was supposed to go.

"Some coaches, even some great ones, don't do all the scouting stuff, but that was something Fitz thought was important, and it's something we've stuck with," Few said.

Dan Monson knew that Dan Fitzgerald and Mark Few were very different people with disparate temperaments and perspectives. But they made it work ... to each other's benefit.

"Those two people are not at all similar," Monson said. "But that was one of Fitz's strengths; he let us develop, let us coach, let us recruit and let us be our own people. Mark thrived under that. And nobody has ever questioned his talent or his will to win or to recruit. Fitz really allowed him to be his own person."

Monson said he learned what it is to be a coach from his father, Don, but he learned "how" to coach from Fitzgerald.

"He had a style that was his and he believed in it," Monson said. "You knew he was in charge and some of the things you knew you wanted to implement and some of them you knew didn't fit your personality. With him, he was who he was, and you knew where he stood."

Grier feels the same sense of gratitude.

"Yeah, he could be tough on you, but he was also really good to work for," Grier said. "He gave us a lot of responsibility that a lot of coaches would never do. I know that all of us got opportunities from him that hundreds of guys would have died to have gotten. And that really says a lot about him."

On Top of the World

Debate remains regarding the Zags' arrival as a powerhouse. A consensus hasn't been reached on the "how," and even the "when" raises arguments.

One theory is that Gonzaga sprung full force on the community of hoop aficionados at the Top of the World Shootout in Fairbanks, Alaska, in 1997. Iconic Dan Fitzgerald had just relinquished the head coaching job to make way for Dan Monson. At best, the staff expected a period of transition ... not national emergence.

The tournament field included a Mississippi State team that had been to the Final Four the previous season, a Clemson team ranked fifth in the country, and a Tulsa club coming off a Sweet 16 appearance.

"Really, we were just happy to be in the tournament," Bill Grier said, recalling that he and Monson and Mark Few were not convinced the Zags could win a game up there. The experience of appearing in that competitive crucible, they reasoned, would be beneficial even if it meant stacking up a few losses.

At the pretournament luncheon, as each head coach made a few short remarks, Monson took a light approach, spicing his speech with a few comical jabs about the growing girth of his father, Don. Once he had the gathering chuckling, he commented: "We're going to just roll through this thing."

It was meant to be self-deprecating, because Monson didn't have much evidence, yet, that his club could rise to the level of these opponents, and listeners yukked it up. Gonzaga? Little Gonzaga? These guys couldn't win the tournament if they gave John Stockton another year of eligibility.

"It turned out to be hilarious," Grier said. "Because that's exactly what we did ... we rolled right through that thing."

In the opener, Tulsa needed a shot at the buzzer to get its first-half point total to double digits, as the Zags owned a ludicrous 34-10 lead.

"We looked at each other in the locker room at halftime like, whew, maybe we're better than we thought we were," Grier said.

An outrageously physical Mississippi State team fell to the Zags by two points in the next one, setting up a national cable broadcast of the title game against Clemson. The Zags dusted them off by 13 points. A national telecast of a Gonzaga win over a top-five team carried a message that could not be misinterpreted: This was a different Gonzaga.

A Minute from the Final Four

Some dismissed Gonzaga's first-round upset of Minnesota in the 1999 NCAA Tournament as a function of lucky timing. The

Gophers had four players suspended for dubious academic practices, giving the Zags a soft mark.

The second-round win over top-seeded Stanford was legitimizing, if for no other reason than the Cardinal players were all smart enough to write their own papers. But it still was open to being minimized if critics sought to mention the obvious home-court advantage for Gonzaga of the game being played in Seattle.

But a win over Florida propelled the Zags to the Elite Eight, where they were within a point with 35 seconds left in the game against eventual national champion Connecticut.

Looking back, coach Dan Monson recalled seeing the bracket laid out ahead of the Zags and he could sense the possibilities.

It didn't matter if all Minnesota's players were available and had earned Pulitzers for their inspired scholastic reports, the Zags would have rolled through to the second round anyway, he said.

"We had the attitude that we could win," Monson said. "It never crossed our minds that we weren't going to win that game. Any of those games, really, including the Connecticut game [in the West Regional Finals]. That was the mindset of that group all the way through. So when we got to Seattle, we walked in the gym like we owned it. We knew it was going to be our day."

Against the Gophers, GU had to focus almost exclusively on stopping star forward Quincy Lewis. They did so by siccing Quentin Hall on Lewis with a tricked-up box-and-1 defense.

The next game, against Stanford, played into the Zags' plans. Stanford doesn't get outsmarted with regularity, but the Zags were as prepared as any team had been when meeting the Cardinal.

"We had played them before, and beat them in the NIT [in 1994], and coach [Mike] Montgomery is a very system-oriented guy," Monson said. "Those same high-low post plays they run are variations of the things that [coaches] Jud [Heathcote] and Stew Morrill ran, and go back in that same family tree that I grew up in. We were very familiar with them."

Play in the West Coast Conference, too, had conditioned the Zags and their staff for quick turnarounds, making them accustomed to having to prepare for a second-round game so hastily. At times in the WCC, the Zags would play back to back ... Fridays and

Saturdays. "That was a very cerebral team we had that was used to turning things around in a short period."

Florida fell on a late GU power tip-in by Casey Calvary. And Connecticut was extended to the final seconds as Quentin Hall again out-played an All-America opponent. That time, it was guard Khalid El-Amin.

As the nation of basketball fans bestowed upon the Zags a permanent place in bracket lore, the players already were bridling at being labeled "Cinderellas" and being thought of as mere sojourners at that level of competition.

They knew a secret that others were yet to learn. It wasn't a fluke. It wasn't a lucky streak. They were that good. They were going to be good for a long time. And they knew it.

CHAPTER TWO

Latter-Day Zags

NBA Can Wait

At six foot 10 and 245 pounds, Ronny Turiaf gets to the basket as if driven by homing instincts. Having been an honorable mention All-American as a junior in 2004, Ronny Turiaf faced a decision. He could make himself eligible for the NBA draft and perhaps collect the outrageous financial windfall that accompanies selection. Or he could return to Gonzaga for his senior season.

Hmmmm, potential riches versus homework, early classes and top-ramen. In a decision that runs counter to contemporary trends, Turiaf opted to return to Gonzaga. His reason supplies a telling testimonial to the power of the spirit that seems to infect Zag players.

"I just love this university so much," said the native of LaRobert, Martinique, in his melodic French/Creole accent. "I love my teammates and I have a great relationship with each of them, especially my fellow senior teammate Brian Michaelson. He is somebody I can really relate to. We've been together so long, I just didn't want him to walk out there alone on Senior Night."

Turning down the shot at immediate wealth so you can be around to accompany a friend on Senior Night?

Sacrebleu.

Although head and shoulders above many defenders, Ronny Turiaf opted to return to Gonzaga for the 2005 season rather than jump to the NBA after his junior year.

"Yeah, I knew that deep inside he wanted me to come back, so I wanted to come back for him and for the university," Turiaf said. "I just knew it was the right decision for me to get my education, to graduate. I felt I had some unfinished business here at Gonzaga, so I wanted to come back and finish it up."

White Nails at Home, Cobalt on the Road

For as much as the Gonzaga program is constructed on the concept of collective effort and selflessness on the court, it's also been a haven for free-thinkers, individualists, iconoclasts, goofs, kooks, flakes, rebels and cosmic spirits.

Zach Gourde (Zag, '03) took pride in being different. On the floor and in the classroom, the effort was exemplary. But he sought personal dimension and depth beyond basketball.

"That started before I got to Gonzaga," Gourde said in the fall of 2004 from Feurs, France, where he was playing professionally, and getting rusty with his English from lack of use. "Back in high school, I always wanted to be sure I wasn't classified as a dumb jock. I had a lot of interests I wanted to pursue and I wanted to have as broad experience as possible."

Basketball was fun, he said, and it continued to be. But it was a game, and as such, a diversion from other significant interests.

"At Gonzaga, I was given the latitude to explore other things," he said. "Now, you wouldn't do anything that would jeopardize your performance or the team interests. But it was a place that's open to allowing different experiences because they've had so many strong personalities there over the years."

Gourde's methods of personal expression varied from the outward (styles of hair and sideburns) to the less visible (toenail polish).

Yes, inside those Nikes, Gourde wore toenail polish.

"A girlfriend painted my toenails back in high school one time," Gourde said. "Once you get known for something, you can't stop doing it. At GU, I had a collection of polish that would have rivaled anything any girl on campus would have had. People would give me polish. Every possible color, especially a ton of blues."

Is the application of toenail polish considered an acceptable pre-game activity?

"Hey, I drew the line at the pastels," Gourde kidded. "You've got to pick your fights, after all, and that's where I drew the line."

GU teammates understood it as one of Gourde's quirks and, given the unvarnished effort and desire he showed on the court, nobody was going to be critical.

"We always said, 'Zach is Zach,'" assistant coach Tommy Lloyd said of the team's understanding of his offbeat means of expression. "He was a character ... totally. He always liked people to know that he's involved in a lot more things in his life than just basketball. And everybody knew he was always, always, a great teammate and competitor.

"Basketball is enough for some guys," Lloyd continued. "But for Zach, it was important for him to explore other areas and be well-rounded. Yes, he was a little different, but in a good way. He brought a lot of character to the team, and a lot of color."

Color, yes. But nothing in pastel.

Mayor of Gonzaga

One of Brian Michaelson's responsibilities was the care and tending of center Ronny Turiaf. Michaelson (organized and efficient), made the perfect roommate for Turiaf, (disorganized and spontaneous).

"We're the only two seniors on the team," Michaelson said before the 2004-2005 season. "I can really help him with his focus and his mental approach to the game, help keep his energy high, keep him focused and in a positive state of mind."

Not to mention keeping an eye on his important documents.

"On the road, we have a lot of times where his wallet and passport go missing for a while," Michaelson said. "He's a little scatterbrained ... only because he's got so much going on and has so many interests."

But with practical, day-to-day matters ... whew, Turiaf needs help.

"Ronny can't keep hold of anything to save his life," assistant Tommy Lloyd said. "He's a real character. I have to hold on to his passport because he can't trust himself to not lose it. He's always losing his wallet and documents. He's got two lockers just jammed with crap."

A team manager once was dispatched to Turiaf's apartment to help bulldoze the empty pizza boxes, dirty dishes and unpaired shoes. "It was just about unlivable," Lloyd said.

But Michaelson has never seen anyone as involved in the campus community as Turiaf, who attends almost every school event, major or obscure, and energetically cheers for all participants.

"People just gravitate to him because of his personality," Michaelson said. "He's so special, he takes time for everybody."

The typical GU fan sees Turiaf racing down the floor with flying braids, or dunking decisively, or pulling off a baseline drive. But they probably have no grasp of the popularity of Turiaf on campus. So, could he be mayor of Gonzaga?

"Oh, probably mayor of Spokane if he wanted; I'm not sure what his public policies are, but in terms of popularity ... oh, yeah."

No. 11 Is Cleared to Board

While Ronny Turiaf was kidded about his absentmindedness and inability to maintain custody of his passport, Brian Michaelson pointed out a former international Zag who actually was much worse in that department.

"Germayne Forbes, who was from England, was 10 times worse than Ronny," Michaelson said. "On one trip, he lost his wallet and his passport and had no form of identification at all."

The trip was soon after the September 11 attacks, and security concerns were high. How in the world, then, did Forbes make the trip with the team?

"You won't believe this," Michaelson said. "They showed the security people his picture in our media guide and they let him on the plane."

From Ball Boy to Role Model

As Adam Morrison recalled, he learned two lessons when he was a 10-year-old ball boy for the Zags: "How to sweep the court ... and how to cuss," he said in the spring of 2004.

As if those life skills weren't valuable enough, Morrison absorbed something beyond housekeeping technique and salty language: He decided that he wanted to be a GU player, and nothing—nothing—was going to stop him, including Type 1 diabetes.

Although his physical challenges drew attention from national magazines as early as his freshman year, Morrison was determined that the focus of his career be on his game and his skills ... not his limitations.

"Really I just try to think of it as a non-issue," he said. "As Coach Few has said, and the way I see it, I don't want it to define who I am as a basketball player. I'm more than just 'The Player With Diabetes.' It's not really my nature to be real open about this, but I'm learning that it comes with the territory."

The incentive to break out of his private nature and share the details of his circumstances is singular: To allow his performance to remind others of the possibilities.

"I've learned to get more comfortable with [discussing health issues]. I've heard from a lot of kids who are in the same situation I'm in, and it's important they see what can be done."

A slackjawed series of opposing coaches saw what Morrison could do, as well. Before the Zags' NCAA Tournament game against Nevada in 2004, Wolf Pack coach Trent Johnson recalled his initial thoughts on seeing Morrison play: "This guy's a freshman?" Johnson said. "He plays like a junior. I liken him to a poor man's Larry Bird. He shoots, he passes it ... he has a great basketball IQ, and he has some real toughness to him."

He didn't take long to put those skills on display, either, starting his career by netting a 15-footer in New York's Madison Square Garden against Saint Joseph's. Then he had 18 points against Maryland, 17 against Missouri, and 20 against Stanford.

All the while, Morrison wore an insulin pump in games and in practice. Two hours before every game, he fortified with a meal of steak and baked potatoes, and during the game, he tested his blood-sugar level nearly every time he came off the floor. He balanced his body chemistry with juice or glucose tablets. But two or three times a game he discreetly pulled up his jersey and gave himself insulin injections.

"It's a very serious illness and what he's been able to do is nothing short of remarkable," Zag assistant coach Leon Rice said. "Every kid with diabetes in the country now looks at Adam as a role model. He gets so much mail that we had to create a special means of handling it. He gets them and takes the time to write back to every one of them. He understands the importance of where he is and what he's doing."

Adam's Mark

Coaches tried to not pressure new arrival Adam Morrison; they counseled him to let the game come his way, and not force anything.

"But the second he got the ball, his natural aggressiveness took over," coach Leon Rice said. "He's a guy who is going to be his own man every step and nobody is going to stop him from doing what he wants to do."

The staff sees in Morrison a well-read and well-rounded intellect who follows the path of many former Zags, seeking to assert himself as an individual outside of his on-court persona.

And that keeps assistant coach Tommy Lloyd busy.

"Adam is a very emotional and fiery guy," Lloyd said. "And he can be argumentative; he'll argue about anything. Coach Few may say something and Adam will say something back. I'll come over and pull him aside and say, 'Okay, let's chat.' I spend a lot of time watching and working with Adam. He's very intense."

Instant Classic

The coach claimed it was a privilege to have played in a game so compelling. And that was the losing coach, Gonzaga's Mark Few. But Arizona's Lute Olson voiced the same sentiments after his Wildcats edged the Zags 96-95 in double overtime to escape the second round of the 2003 NCAA Tournament.

With both teams playing near flawlessly in front of a mesmerized Salt Lake City crowd, the Zags rimmed off two shots in the final seconds that could have meant the upset of the top-seeded Wildcats.

"That was one game when the loss didn't hurt so bad," Few said. "It was just so great to be a part of it. Everybody was throwing out maximum effort, maximum concentration, and playing very, very well."

It was one of those rare athletic contests when the magnitude of it was instantly evident. Each team countered the other's surges, matched the opponent's intensity, and the competitiveness escalated with every possession.

"Everybody involved in it had the sense that it was something special even as it was going," Few said. "The players were so focused, there wasn't any talking going on at all. It was just mutual respect."

Zag Tony Skinner, who had been both the goat (missing a late dunk) and the hero (blocking a last-second shot) of the first-round win over Cincinnati, was a dramatic focus in this one, too, scoring on a put-back at the end of regulation to send the game into the first OT.

Blake Stepp missed the final shot at a win in the second OT, but both he and Skinner finished with 25 points.

"It was just a great, great game," Few said. "It's too bad somebody had to lose it."

I Owe You One

He'll admit it; Mark Few has jeopardized the Zags' chances to win on rare occasions.

"I don't know how many technicals I've had, but it hasn't been very many," Few said. "But I got T'ed from across the floor in a game against Missouri [December 2003 at Seattle's KeyArena] when I reacted to what I thought was a goal-tending call, and it could have changed the game. I almost blew the game for us."

The Zags rallied, though, got the game into overtime and whipped No. 3-ranked Missouri 87-80.

In the locker room, Few had a simple message: "Thanks, guys," he said. "They knew they bailed me out on that one."

No Worries

The 2004 season ended with a disappointing second-round loss to Nevada, but it may have established team records for fewest headaches and most cooperative roster. The depth of the team was such that coach Mark Few claimed he easily could have chosen starters from a pool of 10 players with little or no effect on competitive quality.

But it was the attitude and team deportment that was unique. Especially for a club that finished 28-3 and finished ranked No. 3 in the nation.

"Not one time did we have any locker-room issues, or road issues, or one of those calls in the night," Few said. "We did not have one instance where somebody came in and claimed he wasn't happy with his position or his minutes. Not one time. Not once ... all season."

Is that rare in high-level NCAA basketball?

"Unheard of," Few said.

They Also Serve Who Mostly Sit

Heading into his senior season, Brian Michaelson (Zag, '05) never played more than 13 minutes in a game. He had scored 43 points in his career. But he was named co-captain of the Zags.

"He was all-state in Oregon, a really good basketball player, but he's never played significant minutes," assistant coach Tommy Lloyd said of Michaelson. "He's had a real impact in his own way. For one, he lives with Ronny [Turiaf] and he makes sure he's not late and stays at least somewhat organized."

So, how does Michaelson respond to steady scout team duties? As if the NCAA Tournament were at stake. As if nothing could be more important to him.

"He doesn't just know the other team's plays from his position, but from all positions," Lloyd said. "He learns them so he can jump in and play anything from [positions] 1 through 5. He'll know them all. That's an incredible dedication. Look at it this way, he's our captain because he's such a special kid on so many levels."

Michaelson makes one thing clear, team spirit and good nature is important, but he'd still like to be on the floor playing.

"Everybody wants to play," he said. "If you're at this level and don't have the desire to play, then it's the wrong situation for you. I just feel that I can't let my personal desires to play get ahead of the team. I can't have selfish concerns."

Zach Gourde: Being a Zag

For Zach Gourde, it wasn't as much a recruitment as it was an adoption. He could sense it the second he stepped on campus.

"It felt like I was part of a family from the day I arrived on campus. Several players showed up at my dorm room the first night I got to town and they grabbed me, took me out and started introducing me to people. Right from the start, I didn't have to go through that initial searching out of friends that new students have to go through. From the day I arrived, I had 13 or 14 best friends."

The wins piled up, and the few losses were painful, but Gourde can pinpoint an exact moment when he most completely absorbed the significance to him of where he was.

"It was the passing of Father Tony," Gourde said of the Jesuit priest, Father Tony Lehmann, who accompanied the team to all its games. "That was one of the moments when you look around and take stock. You see what everybody's priorities were and realized they were all pretty much the same as mine. To see what he meant to the program, and what he meant to everybody in it ... those were the same things he meant to me. The man really epitomized what a lot of us want to believe we stand for."

Merci Beaucoup, Cory

Cory Violette's big body, soft hands, savvy under the basket and knack for scoring were critical to the Zags' success. But his skill with languages? Not so great.

"He was so big and so strong, it took so much weight off my shoulders having him in there," frontcourt mate Ronny Turiaf said. "He was great to be around. Except when he tried to speak French. We'd be out there doing individual workouts and I'd try to understand the coaches, and Cory would always be talking in French.

"I'd ask him, 'Cory, won't you please be quiet for a second,'" Turiaf said. "And he'd go, '*Oui, oui, oui.*'"

Casey on Cory

One of the widely held notions was that Casey Calvary's toughness on the young Cory Violette helped him turn into an all-league talent in later years.

"Yeah, I gave him a hard time," said Calvary (Zag, '01). "I tried to work hard with him every day. I always believed in him and he ended up being a great player and having a great career."

Calvary actually saw a lot of himself in Violette, and he wanted to instill (okay, hammer into him) the competitiveness he thought Violette would need to lead the team.

"When he came in, I looked at him as a kid who was a lot better than I was as a freshman; he had a lot of the same tools. He was athletic and strong and had a nice touch from the outside. Gonzaga is a place I take huge pride in, and I saw him as one of the guys who was going shape the future of the program."

*Cory Violette force-fed baskets to the delight of the "Kennel Club,"
so well that the Zags peaked at a No. 2 ranking
his senior season (2003-2004).*

Michaelson: Being a Zag

To Brian Michaelson, becoming a Zag is a process.

"It's kind of something you grow into. When I first got here, I'd see older guys coming back and helping out; you could see the special bond they shared. I wondered, at the time, if it would be like that for me.

"Yeah, it is. I consider everybody who has been here and moved on, those before me, and the younger guys, as good friends. A lot of it seems to have been passed down, generation to generation, you could say. It's the work ethic and the pride in doing things the right way and winning the right way. It's a pride in the fact that nothing is individual, it's about the team. In fact, it's not even about the team, because teams change from year to year ... it's about the program.

"Teams change, but the program is here every year. People who aren't in it probably have a hard time understanding this. I care about protecting the image of this program for the people who played here before me. I know the guys coming up feel the same way for us. That makes this something really unique and special."

Latest Edition of Midnight Madness

For decades, since the days when John Stockton squirreled away a key to the gym and nearly wore the wax off the court, a succession of Zags have found the regular work day insufficient to meet their demand for practice.

Derek Raivio is the latest of the nocturnal skulkers.

"A lot of guys have been hard workers, but I'm not sure there's been anybody who's done more than Derek Raivio," coach Tommy Lloyd said. "A bunch of our night janitors are people who have emigrated from Eastern Europe, and he's on a first-name basis with them. I've come in here late at night after camps and things and he's in here playing one-on-one with a janitor."

Ronny Turiaf: Being a Zag

Ronny Turiaf speaks four languages. But to speak English isn't always to understand "American," especially the dialect specific to college basketball players and coaches. It made the adjustment to life in America difficult in the early stages.

"I just came here as a Caribbean guy new to the American culture," Turiaf said. "I had a hard time listening to my teammates and understanding them. And listening to my coaches, trying to teach me things, I couldn't always understand them."

Being around the team on a daily basis smoothed the assimilation process.

"I don't think people can put a finger on what it's really like at Gonzaga," he said. "Being a Zag is being a Zag, there's nothing else like it. You're around a bunch of guys who love each other, care about each other and who have each others' backs. We're like brothers now, and I know that 25 years down the road, we're still going to be friends."

CHAPTER THREE

The Stockton Mystique

Maintaining Ties

John Stockton, the self-effacing superstar, goes largely unseen in Spokane. It's a place where he's comfortable because the citizens have learned to give him space. But that doesn't mean that he's not around.

"He's here every day," coach Mark Few said. He sees him frequently in the weight room or the gym. Although he's mostly a blur. Few reports that Stockton still "gets after it" in workouts. And he still frequently plays with the Zags during open gym.

"He would have helped Team USA [in the Athens Olympics] if they could have added him," Few said. "He's still that good."

Consider it unsurprising, given his competitive (no, combative) nature, that Stockton "doesn't back down from anybody out there," Few said. There may not be 19,000 rapt Utah Jazz fans slavering over his efforts. But that doesn't matter to Stockton.

"He's all about winning," coach Bill Grier said. "Look, you don't survive as long as he did, at his size, without being a fierce, fierce competitor. And he still is; you see it every time he steps on the floor … playing against anybody."

Stockton's competitiveness can be misinterpreted by those who aren't accustomed to the searing intensity, said Steve DeLong, GU trainer and friend. "Some people get on him a little bit because he's the ultimate competitor. Whether it's Pictionary or the NBA Finals, yeah, it's like it's for the world and he doesn't mess around."

The Stockton Impact

The appearances of former playing greats at some schools are limited to photos in the trophy case and names in the record books.

John Stockton is not just a legend at Gonzaga, he's actually out there on the floor, swapping elbows and blowing past players on drives to the hoop. Contemporary Zags don't watch videos of him to learn how the game is played ... they see it in sweaty flesh and sometimes blood, first hand, on a regular basis.

"He's got a great relationship with our players," Mark Few said. "He's a really, really witty guy, which is one thing that the public doesn't see. So he has a lot of fun with these guys."

The players, of course, elevate their game to tournament intensity whenever he's on the floor, the benefits of which might be seen annually in March.

"It helps all of them, big guys as well as guards," Few said. "They see his professionalism every day; they see his no-nonsense approach and how he values the game. That's probably the best thing. Matt [Santangelo], Dan [Dickau], Blake [Stepp] ... they all learned from him. Richie [Frahm] saw his professionalism and I know that helped him understand what it takes to play in the NBA."

Perhaps Stockton's most sincere gift to the Zags is that he never plays down to them. He gives them his best moves and his game-day effort. They would expect no less, having been schooled in his legacy of unrelenting exertion.

"John lit the torch that's been passed down," Few said. "It's the legend of him having the only key to the gym and how he'd be in here all night shooting. Now, Derek Raivio is in here, and before him it was Dickau and Kyle Bankhead and Richie Frahm. That's an important part of what this is all about."

John Stockton's drive allowed him to leap from Gonzaga to the NBA, where he established the all-time record for career assists.

Steve DeLong said Stockton is so humble that he worries about offending the players with his presence. "He asked me one time: 'Do you think the fellas would mind if I played with them again?'"

Which is not to say that the humility stands in the way of his mugging them in pick-up games and doing whatever it takes to win.

"Oh, he comes right after them," DeLong said. "And they love that more than anything."

Dream Team Day Care

John Stockton had just returned from appearing with the first Dream Team in the Barcelona Olympics. He was well on his way to being honored as one of the NBA's 50 greatest players, and establishing an all-time record for assists.

He was also on his way to elementary school.

Billy Grier, driving down Hamilton Street on the way to work one early morning shortly after the Olympics, witnessed a sight that might be considered rare among Dream Teamers.

"Here's John on the sidewalk walking his kids to school," Grier said. "How many Dream Team guys walk their kids to school? John Stockton did. To me, that says a lot about him."

It says something about Spokane, too, as a place Stockton can walk down a street with his children and not be beset by gawkers or autograph hounds.

"He really appreciates that," said Jack Stockton, John's father. "The people here have been good to him. Around here, he's just another guy. Well, maybe not quite just another guy. Maybe he'll never be just another guy, but as much as you can imagine, they treat him that way around here."

The Stock Market

As a presentable man with impeccable reputation and extraordinary skills, John Stockton could have pocketed unimaginable dollars in endorsements. But Stockton is the curator of his own mystery and has mastered the art of stealth and inconspicuousness.

"He's never wanted that," Steve DeLong said. "And you have to respect that about him."

Some have suggested that Stockton could more broadly spread his image as a positive role model if he sacrificed some of his privacy. But, again, that's not what he's about.

"I tell him all the time, 'You have no idea what kind of impact you could have on people,'" Delong said. "But he does so much that people never see and that I can't talk about. There are [charitable] things he does in Spokane and regionally and in Salt Lake City that nobody has any clue about. And that's exactly how he wants it."

At the root of it, DeLong feels, is a genuine humility.

"I don't think he realizes how great he was, or the perception people have of him," DeLong said. "He doesn't see himself as anything special. In the summers when he was playing, he was always saying, 'I've got to get better for next year; what can I do to make myself better?'"

GU baseball coach Steve Hertz, a Stockton friend, is equally moved by his desire to maintain a low profile.

"Do you have any idea how much money he could have made on endorsements and commercials?" Hertz asked. "He has forfeited many, many millions so that his kids don't have to see the Stockton name every time they turn around. He wants some normalcy in their lives. People can talk about ideals and beliefs, but he's given up millions of dollars for his."

Destined for Greatness?

When the stringy local kid stepped up from Gonzaga Prep to GU, it was met with modest expectations and an absence of fanfare.

"He was just kind of another guy," said Ken Anderson, a senior during John Stockton's freshman year. "We all knew him of course, and John was good. But it certainly wasn't like you could see what kind of career he was going to have. There's no way you could imagine he'd turn into one of the all-time NBA greats."

Defenders had their hands full when John Stockton had the ball.

Even as he ripened as a Zag, Stockton himself didn't have a true feel for where he was headed.

"I remember midway through his senior year sitting and talking to him about the future on a road trip at the Santa Clara Marriott," Anderson said. "And we talked about him trying to find a team to play for in Europe. Can you imagine that?"

Teammate Jeff Condill (Zag, '86) agreed, nobody could have presaged Stockton's development in the NBA.

"Nobody except maybe John," he said. "Everybody talks about how smart he is and how hard he works, but what gets overlooked is what a great athlete he is. He can just flat outperform people in any aspect of athletic endeavor, you name it: baseball, football, anything. If he sets his mind to it, he can get it done.

"He's quick, he's fast; his body isn't big, but he's well put together. That's the only way he could have played 19 years and missed only six games or whatever," Condill said. "We all knew that if he got a chance, somebody was going to have a tough time taking it away from him."

Going for the Gold

Guard Marlon Wadlington (Zag, '88) loved the challenge when John Stockton would be in town and join the Zags for practices or workouts. Speedy himself, he called out the NBA All-Star for a race over 100 meters one time.

"It was close, but I won," said Wadlington, an attorney in Los Angeles. "We went to Jack and Dan's [Tavern] after that, and I gave it to him pretty good. I said, 'I thought you were quick, but I guess not all that quick.'"

Stockton, although never known outside his inner circle for brash remarks, filleted Wadlington with his rejoinder.

"Yeah, but I'm pretty quick to the bank."

Johnny Be (Real) Good

With manpower running short and the 1984 season growing long, a bug swept through the GU roster the week the Zags were scheduled to play host to rival Santa Clara. John Stockton was sick all week and couldn't practice.

"We were all so worn down and feeling miserable, Johnny was probably down to 165 pounds and I was 170 at best," Jeff Condill said. "But Santa Clara was a big rivalry for us. John was so sick he didn't practice at all and we didn't know if he was going to be able to even suit up. When he showed up, he looked like hell."

Stockton suited up, tied on his shoes. "And he absolutely carried us; he had 35 against them and we won," Condill said. "That tells you what kind of a competitor he is."

Assist, Stockton

John Stockton used to tell GU baseball coach Steve Hertz that he wanted to build some indoor batting facilities for the Zags, to help them with preseason and bad-weather training.

"He called me one day and said, 'Coach, there's an old warehouse in the neighborhood that I think we can get and put some batting cages in there, would you go take a look at it?'" Hertz said. "It was just a big, open warehouse, but he bought it. Now there's basketball courts in there and batting cages. It's made such a positive impact on that neighborhood and our program."

So Stockton found an empty place and filled it with basketball and competitiveness. In a larger sense, that's what he did at Gonzaga years before.

Jack Stockton, John's father and co-owner of Jack and Dan's Tavern just across the street from Gonzaga, has seen the crowds of young athletes flocking to the Warehouse.

"It's a really nice place," he said. "They've got the old Jazz court out of the Salt Palace with the old logo on it."

Stockton and teammate Karl Malone each bought half the court when it was dismantled.

"They decided half of it wouldn't do either one of them any good," Jack Stockton said. "So John bought this place to put it in and Karl sold him his half."

Mike Nilson (Zag, '00) has seen its impact many times: A kid wants to get into the Warehouse to shoot around, and John Stockton will go down and personally unlock the door for him.

"And then he'll go in and rebound for the kid," Nilson said. "Even if he's busy or has somewhere he's got to be, just so he can help the kid."

Nilson plays with Stockton many Sundays, and he'll stack his pick-up team with current or former Zags while Stockton will pick a gang of high school kids as his teammates.

"And his team always wins," Nilson said. "It's no coincidence; he just is so incredible at getting the ball where it needs to go and making everybody else better."

In the early fall of 2004, Nilson and Stockton both were coursing after a loose ball ... and both dove to the floor in its pursuit. It was a Sunday afternoon pick-up game, Stockton, in his 40s, was still flying to the floor to collect a loose ball. No fans to see it; no money on the line. No titles at stake.

Why?

"Because that's the way he feels the game needs to be played," Nilson marveled.

This consuming passion for the game is only a part of the unseen Stockton lore. Nilson is even more awed by his understated compassion and thoughtfulness.

"One day, I left the game early because my asthma was bothering me," Nilson said. "He said, 'Hey, let me follow you home to make sure you're all right.' Then, the next day, he called me to see how I was doing. That's somebody who really cares; people don't have any idea what a terrific person he is, so caring, so giving. He's just really awesome to be around."

Garbage Time

Steve Hertz tells a story he thinks reveals more about John Stockton than any NBA record or stats sheet ever could. He was with Stockton once in San Diego on a trip to a baseball game.

Walking down the street, Stockton spotted a beer can on the sidewalk. "He went over, picked it up, and threw it in the garbage can," Hertz said. "There's nobody around, he just sees the trash and picks it up. It's not a big thing, but it shows you what kind of guy he is."

The Stockton Joke Book?

Media covering the Utah Jazz throughout John Stockton's career might be less than convinced about this, but those in the Gonzaga athletic department who know him contend he's a wicked wisecracker.

"He's got a sharp wit," Steve DeLong said. "His senior year we were playing at Boise State and before the game he was popping off, being funny. He never liked to stretch and I got on him, 'Stockton, you need to stretch.'"

DeLong decided he needed to force the issue and started pushing Stockton into a stretching position.

"I strained his back," DeLong said. "I did it to him. I hurt him."

First of all ... do no harm. Isn't that the trainers' credo?

Stockton detected in DeLong the early stages of mortification, and started twisting the dagger, telling him he was going to squeal to the Jesuit fathers that the trainer had tortured him.

"I'm feeling pretty bad about it, and he kept yipping and riding me pretty hard," DeLong said. "He ended up playing in the game ... but oh, I heard about it."

Those not within the radius of his close friendships don't get to see the Stockton humor, as he's always been self-contained and publicly reserved, or, more likely, invisible. Jack Stockton has told the story about how he and John's mother proudly presented him with a letter jacket of his high school, Gonzaga Prep, and John never wore it. Not once. He didn't want to draw attention to himself.

GU alumni director Marty Pujolar counters the popular notion that Stockton is dry and stoic.

"He's one of the greatest smart asses who has ever been through here," Pujolar said. "I've always said the really funny guys are smart, because dumb guys aren't funny. And we all know how smart John is. He used to be an absolute non-stop smartass when he was here."

Before John had his number retired by the Utah Jazz, Jack Stockton was asked if he thought that event might lead his son to open up and say a few words.

"He better, or I'll get his mother to prod him some," he said. "Actually, he's getting better at that stuff."

Stockton's Night

The night Gonzaga retired John Stockton's No. 12 jersey, Steve Hertz brought him into the locker room to talk to the team. Guard

Gonzaga retired the jersey of John Stockton (here with wife Nada), but Stockton himself stays active on the court, often playing pick-up games with Zags.

Kyle Bankhead was charged with the duty of presenting Stockton with a ball signed by the team.

"Bankhead is a man of few words," Hertz said. "But he was great. He said, 'John, I can't express what you mean to all of us. You changed the game; you made it possible for a guy like me to have a chance to do this. Somehow, I'll repay you by doing it right.' John got teary-eyed and Kyle got teary-eyed."

Stockton, Hertz reminded, is a man of even fewer words, but gave an equally emotional response.

"John told those guys that there were a number of players in that room who were better than he was when he was here," Hertz said. "He told them how much of a fan he was of theirs, and how much their good efforts meant to him. It actually meant a lot to all of them."

Zag Myth: Steve Kerr Rejected

The story is told that guard Steve Kerr, who would go on to be an All-American at Arizona and become the NBA's all-time career three-point-percentage leader in a 14-season career, was recruited seriously only by one school: Gonzaga.

And the Zags turned him down.

Kerr confirmed that in interviews while playing for the Chicago Bulls. He said he was told by coach Jay Hillock's staff at the time that they liked him but he "wasn't really quick enough to play at this level."

The reason he was deemed too slow? He was playing in a pickup game against a Gonzaga guard at the time: John Stockton.

"Yeah, guess they missed on that one, eh?" Zag Jeff Condill said. "Didn't hurt my cause, though ... I got to start the next two years."

CHAPTER FOUR

Bracket Busters '99

Clutch Shots

Among the shots that proved most inspiring in Gonzaga basketball history, a couple never made it onto the stats sheets and failed to engender wide public notice. That's because they were made at the end of a practice, and it was coach Dan Monson doing the shooting.

In their final tuneup for the NCAA Tournament West Regional opener in Seattle's KeyArena in the spring of 1999, the Zags finished up practice in their customary manner, with everybody hauling off and hurling shots from midcourt. It's a chance to wind down and have some laughs, as coaches and teammates volley commentary, and bust chops with impunity.

Monson took the last shot, and it was so pure it barely even made a swish. Recognizing it for a fluke, players fired the ball back to Monson for what would surely be a humiliating reprise.

He did it again. All net ... two in a row.

The Zags collected at center court and cheered wildly, certain that Monson's marksmanship was an unmistakable omen of impending success. Heading into perhaps the most important game in school history, against a heavily favored Minnesota team, they understood that, from a national perspective, they were unknowns.

But they knew they could play and they knew they were more disciplined, better prepared, and probably as athletic as any team they'd have to face.

The next day, they scored an upset win over No. 5-seeded Minnesota to trigger a streak of success that took the Zags to the threshold of a Final Four appearance ... with only a five-point loss to eventual titlist Connecticut ending their string of upsets in the regional final.

"Oh," kidded Monson of his long-range accuracy. "That was commonplace."

"Yeah, he couldn't make a jumper to save his life, but he can make half-courters," coach Bill Grier countered.

The half-court competition between the staff and players was a carry-over from the Dan Fitzgerald era. Supposedly, a running tally is kept, but it's usually forgotten by the end of the season.

"It's a pride deal ... the players would hate to lose to us," Grier said. "But for the head coach to make two in a row, at the NCAA Tournament, with all the media there watching and the players excited ... that was a pretty good effort."

Colleje Athaleets

The day before the Zags were to meet Minnesota in the first round of their surprise 1999 NCAA Tournament run, the Golden Gophers had to suspend four players for scholastic misdeeds.

One Minnesota official said there was enough "prima facia" evidence of academic misdeeds to warrant the suspension. ("Prima facia" being Latin for: Caught with pants down.) Apparently, players were having their papers and reports written by a tutor.

It gave the throng of Gonzaga's Kennel Club members invading Seattle's KeyArena plenty of ammo to toss around during the game. The best sign: "Phlunk the Goferz."

The best chant: "Do your homework ... CLAP, CLAP, clap, clap, clap ... Do your homework."

After the game, GU coach Dan Monson praised his team's basketball accomplishments but also its solid academic standing, and noted that the victory over Minnesota "validifies" the Zag concept of the student-athlete.

Monson may have purposely constructed the comical term (a marriage between validates and verifies?) for the sole purpose of forever eliminating himself as a suspect if anyone were ever accused of ghostwriting scholarly papers for his players.

Mixing with Mad Dog Madsen

In the 1999 tournament opener against Minnesota, a harassing defensive effort by guard Quentin Hall shut down Gopher star Quincy Lewis. Against Stanford in a second-round upset, it was slender Mark Spink who helped make a difference by hounding the Cardinal's rugged Mark Madsen.

Spink knew his role ... and it wasn't to be a scorer. With his long arms and fearless demeanor, he was expected to assault Madsen from any angle he could devise. This, after all, was what Spink did best.

"My role is to go in and beat the hell out of somebody and try to get some rebounds and a bucket here and there," Spink said. "A lot of it is just mental toughness; it comes down to who is going to hit first and the hardest. You have to let them know it isn't going to be easy for them."

It was a marvelous challenge for Spink, because Madsen brought the same tenacity to the floor, only he carried it around along with 50 or 60 more pounds.

"If you look at Stanford in those years, even to this day, they are kind of what Gonzaga would like to emulate," Spink said. "They're hard-nosed, bright guys. They're the biggest bully on the block, and at my position, Madsen was the biggest of the bullies."

The Zags won by 12 points, largely because they outrebounded the taller Cardinal 44-31. Spink collected five rebounds, four personal fouls and two felony assault charges in 14 frantic minutes. Madsen was typically powerful, with 15 points and 14 boards.

The Tip of Florida

Florida led Gonzaga by a point with time racing toward the buzzer. At stake was a trip to the West Regional Finals and a shot at a Connecticut team that eventually became the champion of that 1999 NCAA Tournament.

Coach Dan Monson instructed quicksilver guard Quentin Hall to foul when the Gators got the ball in, but he raced over into an impromptu double-team and forced a traveling violation.

Hall was going to take the deciding shot in the final ticks, Monson told them, and everybody else needed to sprint into the post to corral the ball if it caromed off. Which it did. And the quick-leaping Casey Calvary snatched it away from a cluster of grasping hands.

"The ball came off and I got a good handle on it and put it back in," Calvary said of his game-winning tip with four seconds left. "Then we all just scrambled back trying to pick up a man and praying nobody could make some desperate shot."

They celebrated wildly, surfing cresting adrenaline. But few really absorbed what had happened. They had no perspective; no context for the experience. What, then, could possibly be going through their minds at a time like that?

"Nobody had expected us to do anything in the NCAAs," Calvary said. "When we beat Minnesota [in the first round], everybody thought it was a fluke because they didn't have all their guys. The win over Stanford was legit, but then to beat Florida and be one game from the Final Four, given where this program had come from, didn't seem real to us. It was like we were floating on air. The two Sweet 16 runs we had after that weren't the same because we'd done it before. But that first time, it was a feeling I still have a difficult time describing."

Zag Quip

Dan Monson's Zags had just scored their third consecutive upset of the 1999 NCAA Tournament, dumping Florida 73-72 in Phoenix. Center Casey Calvary had tipped in the game-winner.

As were the rest of the Zags, Monson was carried away with the contagious postgame delirium. But he also knew, as he entered the locker room, that it was a time for him to show a measure of coach-ly restraint and control, to channel the Zags' cresting enthusiasm toward the next challenge.

"Okay, what we've got to do now ... " Monson started in earnest exposition and presidential bearing. "What we've got to do now ... aw, hell, I DON'T KNOW what we've got to do now!"

Humble Beginnings

Surely, the Gonzaga team of 1998-99, which advanced to the threshold of the Final Four, gave the staff unmistakable early hints of what it could turn into.

Uh, actually, not so much, no.

That edition of the Zags lost 49-48 at Detroit (against the university, not the Pistons) in early December, and late that month squared off against a Texas-Pan American team that won three games the previous season.

Coach Mark Few remembers the Zags looking like anything but a Final Four contender.

"We were down two at Texas-Pan American, and we dink around and foul the wrong guy at the end; we fouled their best shooter," Few said. "But the guy missed both shots. We're in such a fog, the ball comes off the rim and bounces twice before Casey Calvary gets down on the floor and swats it over to Matt Santangelo who dribbled down the floor and hit a three at the buzzer to win it."

Scared but not beaten, the Zags shaped up and won the West Coast Conference title and tournament before gaining their first national prominence with three NCAA Tournament wins ... an

The focus of Matt Santangelo (Zag, '00) rarely strayed from the game of basketball. Jonathan Daniel/Getty Images

astonishing development to anybody who saw the performance in late December.

"It was hard to believe that was the team that took Connecticut down to the last minute to go to the Final Four," Few said. "So, this was not something we really saw coming."

Playing Down

In the list of major victories that have accrued during the Zags' rise to prominence, a squeaker over Texas-Pan American right before New Year's of 1999 will be overlooked. But not by Casey Calvary.

"Sometimes, it's the weirdest games you appreciate," Calvary said. "We were playing Texas-Pan American one game in Texas and they were ranked something like 305th out of 303 in Division I. We got there and played in one of those gyms that seat about 200 people and they don't even bother to turn on all the lights. It was such a strange environment."

The Zags were scheduled to play at Texas Christian University two days later, and that was the focus of the trip. The Pan-Am Broncos, after all, could hardly be considered much of a threat. At the time, they were 2-10 on the way to a 5-22 season.

The atmosphere and circumstances converged to create a nightmare.

"One of their guys got hot and they took the lead," Calvary remembered. "We were down at the end and they got two free throws. He missed the second. I go to get the rebound and I tripped over one of their guys. But I got the ball to 'Tange' [Matt Santangelo] ... it went through the legs of one of their players ... and he went down and pulled up for a three at the buzzer to win the game."

A loss to a 5-22 team would have destroyed the team's RPI ratings that season, Calvary pointed out.

"That would have killed us," Calvary said. "But we pulled it out. There were no cameras there, no highlights, but it was a huge victory for us. To have Matt make that shot was amazing."

CHAPTER FIVE

Wooing Zags

Left at the Altar

Most observers outside the game probably can't understand the emotional equity that coaches invest in coveted recruits. The courting process may take several years, and strong and lasting relationships grow from the contact. And when a prospect decides to matriculate elsewhere, it creates a very real sense of heartbreak that can linger stubbornly.

Mark Few thought he had the perfect Zag point guard in Luke Ridnour, a coach's son starring at Blaine High School up near the Canadian border on the west side of Washington.

He was tough and quick, heady and creative. He understood the game so well that his distribution of the ball was as if guided by pure instinct. As a GU assistant, Few contacted him early and was unrelentingly vigilant. When Luke finally was ready to sign, Few had just become the head coach, and Ridnour would be his signature recruit.

"I just loved what he was all about," Few said of his obsession. "He indicated early on that he had an affinity for the program. And he knew I thought the world of him. In my first year as a head coach, he was about all I could think about. I thought about him every night."

Washington and Utah had been similarly enamored and also had spent years wooing the slender, tow-headed guard. Belatedly, Oregon ducked in. "Sometimes when you're on a kid for a long time they've heard everything you have to say and get used to it," Bill Grier said. "Oregon came in on him and maybe it all sounded fresh."

Ridnour agreed to become a Duck. And Few was crushed.

"I couldn't sleep, couldn't eat, couldn't do anything," Few said. "It was pure depression."

Grier worked hard to pull Few from his despair, but it took weeks.

"In all the years, there was not a kid he had a better relationship with or put more effort into than Ridnour," Grier said. "For Mark, it was a devastating deal. The kid was such a perfect fit."

Few saw in Ridnour the archetypal Zag, a guy who wanted nothing more than a ball and a place to practice. "We all knew that wherever he went, he'd be a huge success because he was so focused and driven and disciplined," Few said.

He just never believed he'd go anywhere but Gonzaga.

Hi, We're from Gonzzzz...

Dan Monson made his best recruiting pitch, evoking his most charismatic qualities to describe the way Gonzaga provided a mixture rare in college basketball, an environment in which academics and athletics could not only coexist, but flourish. He extolled the wonders of Spokane, and how the GU program was on the verge of sustainable national prominence.

The recruit and his family had seen the drill ... many times. And as Monson picked up speed, the recruit's father sank deeper and deeper into his recliner.

Assistant coach Mark Few quickly recognized that Monson's message was being broadcast on a frequency the father wasn't receiving, so he jumped in as a change-up.

"Dad was over there nodding off; you could see the spiderwebs growing," Few said. "Finally, he just laid back and started snoring. The kid was still there, but it's kind of hard when you're trying to talk to the kid and the dad is sawing logs."

The coaches saw where this was headed, beat a retreat to the car ... and fell down laughing.

"The dad falling asleep on us," Few said. "That was kind of the ultimate compliment on the quality of our presentation."

Where Would Jesus Play?

Leon Rice likes to kid that he once walked into a recruit's living room and saw Jesus Christ. Signing him to be a Zag surely would have landed Rice a lifetime contract from the Jesuits.

Actually, it was an actor who merely played the Prince of Peace in a movie. On a home visit to Tyler Amaya's house in Mount Vernon, Washington, Rice met one of Amaya's friends ... actor James Caviezel, who starred in Mel Gibson's *The Passion of the Christ.*

"I walked in and saw this guy, and to be honest, he looked a lot like John Stockton," Rice said.

Caviezel, a former basketball player at Bellevue Community College, wanted to help Amaya with his decision.

Rice was impressed by Caviezel's interest in basketball, although they also talked about the movie business.

"Did you know he once turned down a chance to do a love scene with Ashley Judd?" Rice asked.

Huh?

"Yeah ... imagine that," Rice said.

The trip might have resulted in some important casting though.

"I told him that if they ever make a movie about Gonzaga basketball," Rice said. "He'd be perfect for the role of John Stockton."

Zag Quip

One of the highest compliments to the Gonzaga program Leon Rice has heard while on the road recruiting came from Missouri coach Quin Snyder.

"I gotta find me some Zags," Snyder said. "I gotta get some Zags, because they're tough."

Buddy Can You Spare a Couch?

Mark Few swears this is true. In the lean years, when the recruiting budget amounted to pocket change and bus tokens, Zag assistants on the road used to not only scout players ... but also recruiters from other schools.

If they could find a buddy from a better-funded program, they'd see if they could bunk in with them to save hotel costs.

"That happened all the time ... 90 percent of the time," Few said. "If they had two beds or a couch, you'd see if they'd let you stay with them. We did it ALL the time. We used to sleep in the car, too."

Dan Monson remembers a time when he and Few sought to expand and increase the recruiting efforts, but head coach Dan Fitzgerald balked at the expense.

"Fitz would say, 'We don't have the budget to send you down there,'" Monson said. "And Mark and I would say, 'Hey, we'll figure it out; we'll get it done cheap.' We would find one of my dad's assistants from Oregon, or an assistant from someplace that we knew, and we had them get a second bed or we slept on the floor."

Wasn't the freeloading a little degrading? "Hey, when you don't know any better, you don't care," Monson said.

After several years of mooching couches, Few and Monson finally went to Fitzgerald and made the point that continuing at one step above vagrancy would eventually start to hurt them in the recruiting process.

"Eastern [Washington] still does it," Few said. "Now we're the ones helping out. Hey, you try to help a brother out on the road."

The other "cost-saving" tool the Zags used, without great positive effect, was the storage of a broken-down Ford Tempo at the house of Fitzgerald's brother, Jim, in San Jose, which the coaches used instead of getting a rental car.

"That thing was such a pain; it had a 30-minute rule," Few said. "Every time I got in it, it would run for 30 minutes and then, like clockwork, would strand you wherever you were at that moment. It was awful."

Did Fitzgerald, also the athletic director, mandate the chronic mooching? "Well, what else were you going to do?" Few asked. "You'd go on the road for 30 days and he'd give you $200. It didn't take long to do that math."

Land of the Giants

Seven-foot prospect Eric Chilton lured Dan Monson and Bill Grier to Kelso, where they discovered a race of giants. It seemed to them that the entire family measured out in the seven-foot range. To accommodate the family's dimensions, every stick of furniture in the house was oversized.

Monson tried to project the image of professionalism, and sell Gonzaga as a big-time program, but he convulsed when he looked over at Grier, dressed in his finest recruiting suit, seated in a living room chair ... and his feet didn't reach the floor.

Drop and Give Me 20

Dan Monson and Mark Few knew that trying to cram two home visits into one day is an energetic enterprise that can go quickly from hectic to disaster. But they had scheduled a stop in Seattle and then hoped to end the day in Tacoma with an attempt to mine the real nugget of the class, Casey Calvary.

Calvary, of Bellarmine Prep, projected a toughness that caused the Gonzaga coaches to consider him their primary target. He had broken an ankle his senior year, and that may have scared off some suitors. Not Gonzaga.

Having done their research, the coaches knew that Casey's father was a former military man. They envisioned him in full parade regalia, starched and polished, helmet glistening, slapping a riding crop across his leg.

Their anticipation of the Calvary visit evolved into anxiety as traffic on I-405 came to a dead halt. Time passed. Apprehension boiled into panic, and they pictured the elder Calvary tapping his watch as the coaches grew increasingly tardy for the appointed meeting at 18:00 hours.

"We were panicking," Few said. "Casey was the main guy we wanted in that class. We really loved that guy and we were sure we were out of it with him because we got caught behind an accident on the highway."

Feeling as guilty as if the MPs had caught them going AWOL, Monson and Few sheepishly knocked on the Calvary door an hour and a half late, ready to be told to "assume the position."

Instead, they discovered that "His dad was the greatest guy in the world, and we ended up getting Casey," Few said. "But the panic and stress just about killed us."

But Officer, I'm from Gonzaga

Fans at games, or those watching on television, always see Mark Few dressed in appropriate business suits like the rest of his coaching lodge brothers. But in the summers or even in the warm days of early fall, shorts and T-shirts are the uniform of the day.

"It's a horror for me to wear a suit when it's hot out," Few said.

On recruiting trips, then, he'd often look as if he were on his way to the beach before pulling his suit out of the back of the rental car and spiffing up.

"I'm at a junior college in California to see a kid and it's got to be 95 out ... just not suit weather," Few said.

In his shorts and T-shirt, he pulled up to a secluded space in a parking lot, reached into the back seat for his dress clothes, and started making the switch from beach bum to respected leader of young men.

"Right at the moment of truth, sitting there in nothing but socks and boxers, I hear this knock on the window."

After nearly leaping out of his skin, Few saw a badge and uniform.

"Here I am sitting in my underwear outside their pool ... I can only imagine what he thinks I'm about to do," Few said. "I explained for about 10 minutes that, hey, this isn't what you think; I'm a college coach from Gonzaga, which, at the time, gave me about zero credibility."

Ah, this is the liability of Gonzaga's competitive anonymity in those days. Nobody recognized him. But it was also an example of the benefits ... nobody made a big deal out of Mark Few getting caught, so to speak, with his pants down.

If it happened now?

"Oh, no, it would probably be on ESPN that night," Few groaned.

Of course, a final analysis of the incident demands two questions of Few:

Did you get arrested? "No."

Did you get the recruit? "No."

Score that a .500 day.

G-O-N-Z ...

They always used to have to spell it out. Whenever staff members would call a recruit, or try to make travel arrangements outside the Pacific Northwest, they had to spell out "Gonzaga."

"Everybody used to ask, 'Gonzales?'" Mark Few said. "All those years, you always had to spell it, or very carefully enunciate."

A team bus once pulled up to an arena security gate and the guard was reluctant to grant admission, having not been familiar with the basketball team from "Gonzales U."

When talking to basketball-literate listeners, they took another approach.

"We would preface anything by saying we were from the place John Stockton went to school," Few said.

And now? "You call somebody and they can tell you who was in our starting lineup the last five seasons," Few said.

It was different then. And not always bad.

"Sometimes you miss those days," Few said. "You could just walk around in anonymity and never have to think about a public persona. Now, we are a public entity no matter where we go because of all the television exposure. It used to be different, and sometimes that was nice."

Zag Myth: GU Enlists Ratball All-Star

As the 1984 season wore on, the Zags wore out. "We lost damn near half our team with injuries," Jeff Condill said. "We didn't have enough guys to scrimmage five on five."

As the story is handed down, the Gonzaga staff recruited a student from the noon pick-up games to suit up and become an official member of the team.

True enough. Gino Cerchiai, now a San Francisco businessman, was hauled out of the intramural leagues and handed a jersey. Two games into the conference season, Gino Cerchiai was suddenly a teammate of John Stockton's.

And because of his humble basketball origins, he became an instant favorite of the students, who would chant "We Want Gin-o" late in games.

"I was one of them, so they liked it," Cerchiai said. "I wasn't some recruited player, I was just like them."

Cerchiai recalled being pulled out of the library by a friend and taken down to the gym to meet with coach Jay Hillock. He was offered a spot and actually saw action in the next game, against Loyola Marymount.

"It really didn't sink in for me until the first night I played," he said. "I ran out for warmups and people were asking, 'What's he doing out there?' It was on a different level than anything I had ever felt. I felt like I was walking 10 feet off the ground."

Not one to be bashful with the ball (his team had won the intramural championship, after all, so he had to have "game"), Cerchiai burped up a shot against Loyola. Missed.

But later in the season he went to the line against Portland facing a one-and-one situation. Cool as you please, Gino the Machino drilled both of them.

"I played a total of four minutes and scored two points that season," he said.

He now helps run the family business, a nightclub in San Francisco, and not only still plays recreationally at the Olympic Club, but he claims to be the Deputy Commissioner of the league there.

Given his history, it's not unlikely that as he plays, he occasionally checks the sidelines, waiting to see if scouts from the Golden State Warriors are there looking for an extra guy to fill out the roster.

CHAPTER SIX

Mark Few

Staying Put

College basketball writers might have a macro key formatted onto their computers so that whenever a high-profile coaching vacancy arises, they can simply hit F3 and a sentence appears touting Gonzaga's Mark Few as a top candidate.

In some ways, it's a remnant of the disbelief that Gonzaga can sustain its success, that it can continue to be an upper-level program capable of retaining top talent. So whenever a marquee position opens, Mark Few's candidacy seems logical.

Except to Mark Few.

"I've never been one of those with the big master plans for career goals," Few said. "I always have—and still do—kind of taken it day by day. If you're lucky enough to have a job like this, you get up every morning and thank God you've got another day to do it again. I've always looked at it like this: I get to work with great guys on a day-to-day basis in the realm of athletics ... and GET PAID FOR IT. Can you think of a better job? Are you kidding me? This is great."

He's heard a chorus of coaches over the years outline their ideal career trajectory, using one school after another as a springboard to a bigger paycheck.

"Just spend one day at a Final Four and you see so many coaches who are out there trying to get jobs," Few said. "A lot of guys are looking for jobs they can stay at for two years and then leave for somewhere else. I would bet 90 percent of the guys in this business are doing that, and maybe 10 percent are content and enjoy what they're doing. That's their deal and I wouldn't begrudge anybody wanting to move on, but I'm just in a great situation here."

From a personal perspective, Few sees Gonzaga as one point in a roughly equilateral triangle connecting his immediate family in Spokane, his wife's family in Boise, Idaho, and his parents in Eugene, Oregon.

His bosses are appreciative and supportive, and the Spokane environment suits his preferred lifestyle—as witnessed by the fact that one of the most prominently displayed pictures in his office is of him kneeling in a stream holding a massive fish that he'd just pulled out of a wild Northwest river. The satisfaction on his face almost leaps out of the frame.

But this is what he hears: You've got to cash in while you can, and they'll turn on you if you don't get out of there. "Some guys are firm believers that if you stay too long, no matter how successful you are, it's only a matter of time before you tick off enough people and they'll come after you."

Few has been able to fend off the arguments for relocation with a couple personal beliefs.

"For me, where I'm at with my family, I really value the quality of life we've got going now, so why change it? Now maybe there's a point where you're not challenged enough or you don't feel like you're getting the same support you were getting ... maybe that changes things."

When other coaches join Few in Spokane for camps and events or games, they sometimes start to understand what is the appeal for him.

"I always hear, 'Hey, it's not so bad up here,'" Few said.

North Carolina coach Roy Williams, who recently uprooted after a long stay at Kansas, had some advice for Few as it regarded professional contentment and career moves.

Coach Mark Few gives Erroll Knight sideline instructions.

"I talked to him about having such a great athletic director and supportive president," Few said. "And he just said, 'Call me before you ever think about leaving.'"

Mr. Few Doesn't Go to Washington

University of Washington athletic director Barbara Hedges fired Mark Few's good friend, Bob Bender, and then looked at Few as a candidate to replace him.

For decades, the UW program had seemed such a slumbering giant, and so ripe for awakening, with a new arena and, of course, the football-fed budget.

Considering the combination of Few's success on a national level and his impeccable regional cachet, he stood out as a prime candidate to bring about a long-awaited Husky reversal.

And Few won't bother trying to dodge it, there was some appeal.

"It intrigued me, sure," Few said of the 2002 vacancy. "Seattle's a great town, it's basically got the same appeal in terms of proximity to family. There's more players there to draw from."

Few and assistant Leon Rice were hashing over the relative merits of the UW opening one day while taking a walk. They bumped into a pair of players, Blake Stepp and Cory Violette.

"We just talked to them, and they're such great kids," Few said. "We realized we had two more years with them and, to be quite honest, I just couldn't leave kids like that. Those were my guys, guys who signed with me as the head coach. I couldn't leave them. I know that's not something that always happens in this profession, and it is probably something that is very important that is missing in the profession ... but I just didn't know how I could bail on them."

Other jobs have held appeal, to the extent that athletic director Mike Roth even has been awed by Few's decisions to stay put.

"Mark has been offered jobs each and every year since he's been head coach," Roth said. "[After the 2003-2004] season there was one that never got to the actual offer stage, but it could have been a seven-and-a-half figure job. Now, that's something that gets your attention. But Mark is not chasing the dollar. I think the Washington job might have been a tough decision for him because it was still in the Northwest and his lifestyle potentially didn't have to change that much. So, I know there have been some that he's had to consider to some extent."

Those close to him, though, haven't felt the ties to Gonzaga fraying at all.

"None of us has ever worried about him leaving," Leon Rice said. "Everybody talks about it, but I don't think we've ever come close. This staff knows how good we have it here. I think we still like to fancy ourselves as young coaches, but I think we really have an old-school mentality. We just love to coach, and see that being at Gonzaga is one of the best places in the world to coach."

But some of the reputed offers could have meant immediate wealth and national acclaim.

"That's not what Mark is about," Rice said. "He's got such a good handle on what's important, and he knows that more money isn't going to make him happier than the lifestyle he has here. We've had friends that have moved on and it hasn't always worked out that great."

Some of Roth's administrative counterparts around the country question how he can manage to keep Few, and warns that there's a futility to trying. Eventually, they say, the big money will reach him and shake him and ultimately uproot him. Roth, happily, points to the fact that Few is still on the payroll.

"It's great to realize that not everybody is focused solely on how much money they can make," Roth said. "If he eventually leaves, it will be to a place that is the right fit for him. Right now, he's shown that Gonzaga is the right place for all the right reasons. He knows we have limitations and we know we have limitations, but right now, it's the right fit."

*Mark Few coached the Zags into the NCAA Tournament
in each of his first five seasons.*

Mind Games

Fear, suspicion, dissatisfaction ... yeah, these are part of a coach's psychic repertoire. But Mark Few can pinpoint one that rises above all others as a coach's prime mental disorder: Paranoia.

"Coaches always operate from some level of paranoia—at least slight to moderate. No matter what level you're at, you always think that the bubble is about to burst," Few said. "The ship is going to sink, or a meteor is going to hit the gym. That's what motivates you; we've got to get better guys, we've got to work harder. You can't just stay still because everybody else is improving. Now, we've entered an area of facilities improvement, which was lagging behind the success of the program. But you're always looking at something you've got to improve. That's part of being a coach."

Because if you think nobody's coming after you ... you haven't been reading the sports pages.

A Good Bargain

Dan Fitzgerald remembered hiring Mark Few as a graduate assistant in 1990, when his resume was not exactly bulging with glowing achievements.

"He was a junior varsity coach at a small Oregon high school," Fitzgerald said in a 2000 interview. "He was making $1,500 when we got him and I tried getting him bartending jobs just to keep him going. And if he had a dollar for every time I yelled at him, he'd be a lot wealthier."

It didn't take long for Fitzgerald to see the relentlessness and determination that would be the force behind Few's advancement.

"Of the guys who worked for me, he turned over the most rocks," Fitzgerald said. "He's a scrounger who would go out there and mine some good guys. And the thing I really loved about that guy, if you ever tried to bully him, man, he'd shove it right back at you."

You Should See His Brother ... Kung

Mark Few's name gets tossed into the pile of possible candidates anytime a hot job arises around the country. But he wasn't always that well known ... even on the Gonzaga campus.

At a time when Few was the second assistant behind Dan Fitzgerald and Dan Monson, he was interviewed by a cub reporter on the GU school newspaper.

The article was a flattering personality profile of the young coach out of the Oregon high school ranks. It outlined his dedicated studies of the game's strategies, his skills as a scout of opponents' tactics and tendencies, and his aggressive and exhaustive recruiting practices.

One problem: Throughout the story, he was called "Mark Fu."

Mark Fu.

Game Face

Nobody questioned Mark Few's dedication to coaching. But his response to a nasty car wreck offered conclusive proof that he'd practically crawl through broken glass to get to work. While he was an assistant to Dan Fitzgerald, Few and his wife, Marcy, were in a crash so severe that it could have taken their lives.

Within a few short days, Few showed up at practice wearing the scariest Halloween mask imaginable. Except that it wasn't a mask. It was his face, bruised vivid hues of yellow and purple, and held together with more stitches than a softball.

Unable to move at more than a slow shuffle, with a face still bloated from swelling, Few saw the effect his appearance had on the players.

He told them: "Just call me the Elephant Man."

They laughed and went back to work. Few was in pain, but there was work to do.

Directing Dan

Coaches' personal methods of motivation vary over a range as vast as their offensive and defensive schemes. There are screamers and schmoozers, needlers and wheelers, organizers and administrators. All aim at getting players to recognize their potential, and to help them meet it to the fullest extent.

According to assistant coach Leon Rice, Mark Few is expert at "finding what pushes your buttons and motivating you through your own competitive spirit."

The best example?

"One that I was able to witness from start to finish was with Dan Dickau," Rice said. "When Dan came here from Washington, the knock was that he wasn't tough enough. We never thought that at all, but that was kind of the word we got out of Washington.

"Mark was never malicious or demeaning, but he reminded Dan about that, and I think that was a key to really bringing out Dan's super-competitiveness."

Same Job, Less Spit

As expected, changes were few when Dan Monson turned the Gonzaga job over to Mark Few. Schemes and protocols and long-held procedures remained in place. But Monson and Few were different men with different approaches, and the players at the time noted it in specific ways.

"Coach Monson motivated us with the angle of proving to the world we have a good basketball team," guard Matt Santangelo said at the time of the change. "Coach Few has a different challenge because we've already proven to the world we're good, and now he has to defend that."

As is generally the case, their approach is defined by their personalities. Few coached with different tone and volume.

"It's obvious they've got different temperaments," guard Richie Frahm said. "Coach Few is laid back, and Coach Monson will get in your face and spit all over you."

Positive Feedback

Steve Hertz, GU's former baseball coach, travels with the basketball team in his new role as athletic relations director. So he watches coach Mark Few, and he's pinpointed a single technique he believes separates Few from the mass of coaches.

"If you watch the way he reacts, it's amazing," Hertz said. "Whenever something bad happens, a bad call or a turnover or a mistake that could cost them the game, he claps. He claps his hands at the player. He mentally dominates every negative situation with a positive reaction.

"There's a simple but important psychology there," Hertz said. "You look at the pressure he's under, to be able to respond like that is amazing. Players hate to make mistakes; they hate to let anybody down. For them to look over at the coach and see that he's encouraging him, that's a huge thing to players."

CHAPTER SEVEN

Father Tony

The Soul and Spirit of Gonzaga

As the Gonzaga men's basketball team ascended the national rankings, few outside the program understood the relevance of the bearded man seated at the end of the bench flashing a beatific, if slightly mischievous, grin.

That was the Reverend Anthony Joseph Lehmann, better known as Father Tony. The extent of Father Tony's constituency, though, was witnessed by the response when he passed, in 2002 at age 73, of complications from leukemia. No church in town was large enough to handle the throng of friends, so the Rosary Service for him was held in "The Kennel," home of the GU basketball team.

It was more appropriate there, anyway.

Officially, he was the university's alumni chaplain, and as such, he officiated weddings and wakes and baptisms. Mostly, he was a tireless conveyor of good will and wisdom. His friends called his work a "ministry of friendship." And if that was his job description, he was outrageously successful.

He traveled so frequently in his duties that he had a mock business card printed: "Have Chalice, Will Travel." And for 20 years his travels included road trips with the basketball team.

Coaches and players arrived and departed, but Father Tony was ever present ... same smile, same caring attitude. He was there when the team struggled to win eight games all season; he was there when the team rose to the NCAA's Elite Eight.

"He was a man who had more goodness in him than anybody," said Dan Fitzgerald, the former GU coach and athletic director who long ago invited Father Tony to join the team on the bench. "For the college kids, with all their ups and downs, he was the guy they always came to. They trusted him with everything. I saw the things he did, and he did more good for kids than anybody I've ever been around."

Lehmann was conversant on any topic, secular, sacred, political, athletic ... and certainly geographic. While others in the team's traveling party would stumble gruffly down the concourse for early morning flights, Father Tony would be the first at the gate, alert and happy, eager to chat.

He would look into a person's eyes and ask, "How are you doing?" And he was one of the rare people who listened and cared about the response. Conversations with Father Tony ended with his own unique sign-off: " ... to be continued."

It was delightful turn of phrase ... so full of promise and expectation. It made talks with him feel like serialized cliffhangers, leaving one eager to see him again and discover where the next discussion would head.

It could be any topic, of course, because of his interesting background. Born in Illinois, Lehmann had traveled the world, finding his calling after being spiritually moved by a visit to a leper colony.

For 16 years, he lived as a sequestered monk in a mountain hermitage in Europe. He and his brothers spoke only once a week. Those who knew him later were convinced that he used that time to save up all the counsel and advice and good cheer he would need to dispense at Gonzaga.

"He was a lightning rod for goodness," Fitzgerald said at the time of Father Tony's passing. "After a guy had a bad game, or maybe I was hard on somebody, the next morning at the airport, you'd look around, and you know who he'd be sitting with? That kid. You know, you see guys lose, you see guys fail, he always gravitated to those guys."

Father Tony experienced the ultimate of sonic extremes, going from the silence of the hermitage to the institutionalized mayhem of Gonzaga games in The Kennel. Yet he was comfortable in any environment.

Fans and all but the closest of friends had no notion of the severity of his illness. He didn't want them to worry.

And all the way to the end, Father Tony Lehmann remained consistent: Every conversation concluded with his promissory: " ... to be continued."

The Gymnastic Jesuit

Alumni director Marty Pujolar worked with Father Tony for 20 years, and never lost his amazement over his friend's most famous stunt.

Father Tony would take a dollar bill and fold it in the middle so it would stand on its side. He would take one foot off the ground, bend at the waist, without touching the ground with his arms, and pick up the dollar bill ... with his teeth.

"It was incredible," Pujolar said. It paid off for Pujolar at 10-1 odds one night in a bar when a corpulent drunk bet he could match Father Tony's flexibility. "He fell flat on his face."

The payoff was in question, of course, because Father Tony "wanted to give the guy back the money," Pujolar said. "I said, 'Forget it, he was a jerk and this will buy beer.'"

CHAPTER EIGHT

GU—
Guard University

Idol Time

As a kid, Dan Dickau evaluated himself realistically. He tried to project what his size would be, and what he could do, given those constraints, in the game of basketball. He overlaid those mental projections upon the man he most sought to emulate, John Stockton. And when he detected physical similarities, he knew he had a chance in the game.

"It made me think it was all possible for me," Dickau said. "This guy was the size I figured I'd be when I was done growing, and he's had an unbelievable career. It meant I had something I could work toward."

After transferring from Washington, Dickau faced a rare reality for a young athlete, the chance to actually compete with the icon, to go down to the gym and test his crossover move on John Stockton, to not only study at the knee of the master, but to swap elbows and fight through picks to get a hand in front of his jumpers. This was not poring over old game films to pick up clues to the craft, this amounted to individualized seminars. This is like Stephen Hawking showing up at a GU physics class and swapping formulas with a bunch of sophomores.

Dan Dickau (Zag, '02) transferred from the University of Washington and ended up as a first-team All-American for the Zags.

"Playing against him every day was an awesome experience," Dickau said. "What you saw was a veteran who still played hard in pick-up games, doing whatever it took to win. I spent a lot of time with him, especially my senior year. I would meet him down at the gym in the mornings and shoot with him. The thing that struck me was his dedication to the game; although he'd been at it so long, he still worked so hard. It was an incredible thing to see."

Early Influences

When Dan Dickau arrived at Gonzaga, facing a redshirt year because of the rules governing his transfer from the University of Washington, he felt immediately at home because of his room-mate—Richie Frahm.

"We had been friends since high school," Dickau said, noting the two were from the southwest corner of Washington state. "We grew up in the same area and had played and worked out together, so that made the transition pretty easy for me."

But a redshirt athlete finds himself in an uncomfortable limbo, a part of the team, but not a complete contributor. Especially for a new transfer, it can create a sense of isolation.

Assistant Tommy Lloyd took care of that.

"He was there at the gym for me literally every single day," Dickau said. "Sometimes when you're a red shirt, it's easy to get lost in the shuffle because the staff is focused on winning games. They can't all be tuned in to the guys who aren't going to be playing minutes until the next year."

But Lloyd was. He was in his ear, talking him through the parts of his game that needed work, sure, but also showing a level of concern that Dickau needed to feel at that time.

"He had a huge impact on me, taking that much time, working with me," Dickau said. "That was really important to me."

NBA ... Via Spokane

Dan Dickau gets asked the question frequently. Would he have made it to the NBA if he'd stayed at Washington and not transferred to Gonzaga?

"I think that the way I work on my game, I'd like to think that I would have had a chance anywhere I went," he said. "But would it have been harder? Yeah, I think it definitely would have been. At Gonzaga, I was able to get in a situation and a system that really helped my skills shine and develop. I felt that they definitely accelerated my learning curve once I got there."

But the motivation? That was going to tag along no matter where Dickau attended school.

"Mostly, I push myself just because I love basketball," he said. "Growing up, a lot of kids want to play in the NBA. But you've got to figure out that you have to go to high school first and have to figure out how much you have to do to succeed there. Then you do the same in college; what do I have to do to play against guys who are bigger and stronger?

"I've never shied away from the obstacles that were in the way, wherever I was," he said. "That includes now. My first two years in the NBA had some ups and downs, but I still love basketball and I still want to be a successful player at this level."

Dan Dickau: Being a Zag

Dan Dickau is one of those players, having transferred from Washington, who can evaluate programs from different perspectives.

"GU gets a different kind of player, sometimes a guy who has been overlooked by other schools. Although, now, they're getting some of the top kids. Still, they're selective with who they want. It's generally a guy who loves playing basketball, who generally understands HOW to play basketball, who wants to get better and will do what it takes to get better. These are guys who want to be coached and who don't mind the criticism you have to get sometimes from coaches who are helping you grow as a player."

By being involved in the evaluation process, players have personal equity in making each newly minted Zag a success ... another step toward closeness and camaraderie.

"One thing that is pretty cool is the way coaches allow players to take such a part in the process. When they bring a recruit onto campus for a weekend, they'll flat out ask you to be honest and let them know if you think the kid would fit in, was he the kind of guy you could see yourself playing with for the next couple years? When I was at Washington, sometimes we didn't even know who was being recruited until they showed up the next year and started playing. We were like, 'Who's this guy?'"

Not a Bad Likeness

From the start, Bill Grier saw qualities in Dan Dickau that reminded him of someone special: John Stockton.

"There's that same fierce competitiveness," Grier said. "He will not lose. His wife, Heather, has some pretty entertaining stories about playing Monopoly with him. Whether it's playing cards or on the golf course, wherever, he's fiercely competitive."

Dickau heard chants and barbs at every venue as hecklers assailed his thick storm-cloud hair or made profane alterations to his surname. If it ate at Dickau, he never let it show.

"He is his own guy," Grier said. "Nothing bothered him. He is a guy with a great inner peace and strength about him. I think the reason is, first and foremost, that he's a very strong Christian. He looks to his faith quite a bit, and that's what gives him that peace. His faith is probably as strong as any kid we've ever had here."

In Step with Blake

Blake Stepp had in his possession an extra-sensory capacity required of gifted point guards: Mental telepathy.

"I could almost play with my eyes closed," forward Ronny Turiaf said. "He could get me the ball where I needed it almost like he was in my head. The ball would always be there."

Point guards with vision and an eagerness to distribute the ball are any big man's best friends. But Turiaf called Stepp a pleasure to be around. And the two, the laconic Stepp and the loquacious Turiaf, benefited from each other's skills in ways that had nothing to do with assists or entry passes to the low post.

"I learned so much from him about the game," Turiaf said. "And I think he learned from me about how to express himself. He's not a guy who talks so much, and I would give him a hard time and kid him so he had to talk some."

All the time? "Every day."

One Tough Zag

Blake Stepp had a reputation for saying little. That's probably because he had to clench his teeth and wince so much, playing through pain.

"I remember him playing one game with a 102 fever," coach Bill Grier said. "The year after Dan [Dickau] was gone, we were so reliant on Blake to carry us, and he knew it. If he played well, we'd win. That's how much we were riding on his shoulders."

At the end of Stepp's freshman year, doctors found a micro fissure at the base of Stepp's femur. After an operation, it was considered wise for him to sit out.

"But he wanted to play with Dickau during Dan's senior year," Grier said. "He worked through it, but of course, he didn't have the pop and he was really dragging, having trouble going more than 20 or 30 minutes in practice. But that's how he was; he had some problems, but he also always found ways to play through it."

As has been the case with so many of the other guards that have made their way through Gonzaga, Stepp was driven by a heightened sense of competitiveness.

Blake Stepp (Zag, '04) continued the string of gifted guards at GU, earning second-team All-America honors.

The card games were legendary. Dan Dickau roomed with Kyle Bankhead and Richard Fox his senior season, which meant running games of poker and cribbage. Nonstop, continuous, and fiercely competitive.

Blake Stepp was involved, too, as Dickau's prime opponent.

"It was extremely competitive, especially between Blake and me," Dickau said. "We played golf every weekend, too. We had kind of an unannounced, silent rivalry that was pretty cool. We're both really competitive. And I'm kinda quiet and he's REALLY quiet. But we really got after it."

Who won in golf? "Me," Dickau said.

The Santangelo Drive

Gather some of the great guards— John Stockton, Dan Dickau, Blake Stepp, Matt Santangelo—and you'd generate about as much conversation as a mime's convention. The common thread is not their verbal restraint, but their drive and focus.

Maybe these guys have too much on their minds to spend time on chatter. Ryan Floyd arrived as a walk-on from a tiny school, while Matt Santangelo was a star waiting to emerge. But Floyd could see even then why Santangelo would turn into one of the best Zag guards.

"He was just so much more focused than anybody," Floyd said. "I was there fighting to make the team, and he was kind of the Golden Child, but he worked so hard and was so focused. He was obviously a lot more serious about basketball than the rest of the bunch, which we all totally respected."

Santangelo was gifted physically, too, with the vertical capacity to play the game somewhere between the rim and the roof, but also the ball skills and shooting range to pull up and bury one in your face.

"He was as athletic as any guard we've ever had," Bill Grier said.

Casey Calvary, an intense customer himself, was awed by Santangelo's single-mindedness. "He was always really serious about his game; always focused on achieving in the game," Calvary said.

"And not just on the court, but he'd read the magazines and watch all the basketball games he could."

Part of the drive, Mark Spink felt, was the product of the expectations he faced. "He was serious, and rightly so," Spink said. "There was tremendous pressure on him in his years at Gonzaga. He had to be in the gym, or he had to be the one talking to the media. He was always in the spotlight and that's a lot of pressure."

See the Writing on the Wall

Kindred in their preference for Friday night shootarounds in the quiet gym over partying and carousing, Mike Nilson and Matt Santangelo roomed together, and helped the other stay focused on their primary interest: Hoops.

Santangelo as a roommate, Nilson said, was: "Intense."

"He was always so hard on himself," Nilson said. "If he had a bad game, he'd take it really hard. That's probably part of why he was so good; he had such high expectations for himself."

Santangelo's self-motivation wasn't restricted to subconscious prodding. He actually left notes to himself.

"He would write out motivational sayings and put them on the bathroom mirror," Nilson said. "And then he'd make posters with sayings on them. Big things, like arts and crafts projects, and put them on the wall. It was pretty impressive."

An Animated Pair

The instant transformation of Richie Frahm and Mike Nilson from genial teammates to lethal adversaries the second they stepped on the floor caused coach Mark Few to recall a similarly schizophrenic twosome from Saturday morning television.

"Those two guys always reminded me of that cartoon where the sheepdog and coyote are really polite to each other, say good morning, and then they punch the clock and then just beat the living daylights out of each other until it's time to clock out for the day," Few said. "That was Richie and Mike. They had the most unbelievable battles; no blows were ever thrown, but the battles were incredible."

Coaches, of course, did nothing to discourage the ferocity of the competition, knowing that the players were co-dependents, enablers, pushing the other to game-level intensity every afternoon.

"They'd have claw marks and open cuts after practice, and their jerseys would be all ripped up," Bill Grier recalled.

At times, the battle of wills overtook and obscured whatever might have been the focus of the drill, or even the tenets of fundamental basketball. This was something different entirely.

"When the two of them went after a loose ball, it sometimes ended up not being an issue about the ball at all," coach Tommy Lloyd marveled. "Richie might have Mike in a headlock and Mike would have Richie's body wrapped up while the ball was nowhere even near them."

And Frahm, of course, then returned to the scene of the crimes in the evening to refine his shooting mechanics. But it wasn't just mindless rote, taking shot after shot to improve by repetition alone.

"If you watched Richie work, it was exactly what you'd wish every player did," Few said. "The effort and intensity—even out there by himself—were so much that he'd just be dripping sweat. What was important was that he did everything at full speed, so it was like the shots he would get in the games. Not that half-speed stuff."

Having gone undrafted, Frahm faced long odds in his attempt to find a clawhold on an NBA roster. But those who had been awed by his dedication and indefatigable workouts had no doubts.

"People sometimes questioned him staying at it, but not us," Few said. "We always said, 'Hey, don't count this guy out.' That's why there's nobody more deserving of being in the NBA now. Richie is self-made ... so driven, so confident and so tough that he just proved himself every step."

Welcome to the Jungle

Supposedly, it's a rebounding drill. But the fact they call it "The Jungle" offers a hint that more primitive measures are involved. A basketball is somewhere in the scene, and it takes place on the court and surrounding environs. But the rest might turn into WWF action.

"One time Richie [Frahm] had me in a headlock on the floor and I ripped his jersey off," said Mike Nilson, former Zag who went on to serve as the team's strength and conditioning coach. "Richie was great because he wasn't somebody who looked at himself as a team star who wouldn't want somebody to mess with him. He'd just say, 'Bring it on,' and he'd get after it just like everybody else. That's what made the team so great, and so hardworking, when one of the best players has an attitude like that."

Doesn't applying a full-Nelson (or, in this case, full-Nilson) to a teammate tend to lead to hostilities?

"Nah, Richie and I would just get up and say, 'Hey, way to hustle,' to each other."

Takedown, Frahm

Richie Frahm was such a competitive basketball player it launched a short-lived wrestling career. When serving as an assistant coach, former Zag player Scott Snider acted as an official for a short scrimmage at the close of a practice Frahm's junior season.

"Richie's team ended up losing and he didn't appreciate one of my 'no calls,' evidently," Snider said. When the six-foot-nine Snider came into the locker room, Frahm blindsided him and wrestled him to the floor with a stone-cold smack-down move.

"Richie and I got along and still do," Snider said. "But this goes to show Richie's competitiveness and his hatred for ending up on the losing side."

Ryan Floyd arrived at GU before Frahm and, in essence, battled him for the same position and playing time. He immediately saw Frahm's steeled will.

Richie Frahm was another Zag whose hard work and dedication paved the way to the NBA. AP/WWP

"He had talent, sure, but he worked so hard," Floyd said. "We really got after it in practice; there were confrontations and a few punches thrown once in a while, but there were never hard feelings afterward. Just a lot of respect."

Mike the Barber

Mike Nilson, when not busy mugging teammate Richie Frahm in practice, served as the unofficial team barber. While he did the clipping, he expected the customer to do the clean up. One time, hair was left on the floor, and coach Dan Monson threw the team out of the locker room.

"We had to dress in the stands for a while, trying to cover up the best we could when we changed clothes," Nilson said. "One practice, Casey Calvary popped off a little bit and Mons got after him. Casey fired the ball into the stands and Mons told him to go get it."

This could have been a showdown of strong wills, a power struggle. But Calvary defused it with humor.

"Casey," Nilson recalled, "just told him, 'Sorry Coach, I was just trying to put the ball in our locker room.'"

From Pain, a Connection

Mike Nilson harbored a walk-on's mentality, always trying to prove himself, always looking for ways in which he could feel discriminated against. The slights, real or imagined, were used to stoke his competitive fires.

When he looked at coach Dan Monson, he detected little empathy for his circumstances, and the two butted heads on occasion.

In the 2000 season, as a senior, Nilson tore his Achilles' tendon ... a serious injury.

In that stage of post-surgical self-pity all athletes feel, Nilson received a phone call. It was from Monson, then coaching at Minnesota.

"He told me some things that were really important to me, things that showed he really cared about me and my health and my career," Nilson said. "I got real emotional and he got real emotional, and I learned a lot about him that I never knew. He'll never know how much that call meant to me."

Making the Most of His Gifts

Kyle Bankhead starred on a state championship basketball team at Walla Walla High, but recruiters were cool to his prospects. The Gonzaga staff liked him, but the consensus was that he was not a Division I talent.

All he did was end up starting on the 2003-2004 team that peaked at the No. 2 ranking in the nation.

"He was a walk-on with no scholarship offers," Mark Few said. "But he was so strong, and such a phenomenal competitor. And he was just tough, tough, tough ... one of the toughest kids we've ever had, mentally and physically."

And hardheaded. Early in his GU career, Bankhead suffered what the staff was sure was a concussion. Bankhead wouldn't allow them to substitute for him.

"He wouldn't admit he was hurt," Few said. "When you say he was one of the toughest all-time Zags, that's really saying something."

When told of the compliment, Bankhead predictably demurred.

"It's not that big a deal," he said. "I can not imagine being anything different. I think that's the way you're supposed to be."

Bankhead always knew, regardless of what others may view as his shortcomings, he could shoot the ball. And the Bulldog staff discovered it, too.

"He hit so many dagger shots for us, huge shots that changed or secured so many games, but he never really got enough credit for it," Few said. "He might hit the three that took us from four points up to seven points up. It might not be the buzzer-beater, but it was every bit as decisive as a buzzer-beater in the context of the game."

Bankhead wasn't given his scholarship for time served; he earned it on the floor, despite his humble start as a Zag.

"He became a huge part of this run of success," Few said. "He was here five years and we'd been ranked every year of his career; he probably spent the majority of his career ranked in the top 10 or 15 in the country. He was truly a mainstay for us."

For a hardheaded walk-on from Walla Walla, that's a pretty impressive legacy.

Wizard of Westwood

Harrington, Washington boasts a population of 482. They're mostly wheat farmers, although the region did produce another important export ... Ryan Floyd.

Off the tiny, consolidated Sprague-Harrington team, Floyd was star for a day in one of the Zags' most historic victories, a 59-43 bruising of UCLA at Pauley Pavilion in December of 1999.

"You wish there were a lot more of those," said Floyd, a Spokane pharmaceuticals salesman. "That was a special game for me. That was the cool thing about our team; one person could step up and have a big game at any time. My role was never to take a lot of shots, but in this game, I kind of got my rhythm and started knocking down some shots. The coaches saw I was hot and they told me to go out and let it fly."

At the time, the 43 points was the fewest ever by a UCLA team on its home court.

Those fond of hammering events into metaphors for larger circumstances would have a party with this game. To have a walk-on from a Class B school come out and be personally responsible for GU defeating the once-mighty Bruins at Pauley Pavilion might serve as the ultimate episode of quintessential Zagness.

"Ryan Floyd just took over that game, totally," coach Mark Few said. "It wasn't even close."

Years later, Floyd still isn't sure he fully fathoms all that transpired.

"You know, everything that happened seemed to go by so fast; even all the tournament success. Sometimes it hits you and you have a hard time believing it all happened. I know sometimes I go back to Harrington and go in that little cracker box gym, and to think of some of the great places we played, the huge arenas, it's hard for me to believe."

Kyle Dixon ... Gamer

As a player and coach, Scott Snider watched countless Gonzaga games, and he isn't sure that there's been a better clutch player than the point guard from his playing days ... Kyle Dixon (Zag, '96).

"He never had the best jump shot or the greatest free-throw percentage," Snider said of the Sisters, Oregon native. "But he always stepped up and hit big shots in big games. The first game in the Spokane Arena against Washington State was one. It was a back-and-forth game, and Kyle got fouled with no time left on the clock and us down by two. He went to the line with nobody on the lane, and he made both shots. Unfortunately, we ended up losing that game."

But it certainly wasn't because of Dixon's efforts.

"He had some great battles with Santa Clara's Steve Nash, too," Snider said. "Kyle could only go to his right and everybody knew it. Teams would try to force him to go left, but he somehow was able to end up beating them going to the right anyway."

CHAPTER NINE

The '94 Wild Bunch

Covering the Line

The coaching staff knew that the class of '94 team was a collection of rascals and partiers. But they also were great students, hard workers and individuals who meshed their talents into the school's first postseason tournament team at the Division I level.

"The enthusiasm and energy those guys had really kind of put life back into the program," said Dan Monson, an assistant at that time. "The thing about that group is I don't know if they knew where the line was, but they sure knew how to cover up the line. They never got into trouble. They always answered the bell, they always worked hard, they did well in class and practiced hard. You knew they were crossing the line, but it never got to your desk."

The core of that group had been redshirts during the dismal 8-20 season of 1989, and by the time they were done, they were in the NIT.

"We had been coming off a tough time and we needed a little personality," Monson said. "They kind of had the personality of their head coach [Dan Fitzgerald], too. He kind of felt that, 'Hey, I don't care what you do if you get the job done.' We kind of had to smile at them because we knew they were having a lot of fun."

*Coach Dan Fitzgerald was not always this calm and
controlled on the Gonzaga sideline.*

Pioneer Zags

The 1994 Gonzaga team that was the school's first to win a West Coast Conference title also may have established a school record for closeness, competitiveness and carousing.

"Fitz said it was a collection of the most competitive guys he'd ever seen ... but also some of the smartest," point guard Geoff Goss said. "I don't know if that's true, but that's a combination you don't often see. And you also don't see teams as close as we were. All those guys: Jeff Brown, Marty Wall, Jarrod Davis, Jamie Dudley, Matt Stanford ... we were all in each other's weddings."

In retrospect, the basketball talent of the team may have been overlooked because of the strong personalities involved. Brown was the National Scholar Athlete of the year with a 3.64 grade-point average, but he also pumped in 21.1 points a game to lead the WCC in scoring. That is a combined numerical anomaly almost unheard of in Division I basketball.

Goss recalled his first season at GU when he was part of a red shirt team that included Davis, Stanford, Wall, Scott Spink and Eric Brady. "The first scrimmage, I think Jarrod had 52 points and we beat the varsity by about 50," Goss said. "It was incredible. Jarrod had about 10 threes and Brady had 30-some points. It was one of those crazy deals, but we all thought, hmmm, we may have something special going here."

Different Games

Ten years after playing its last game for coach Dan Fitzgerald, as the most successful Zag team up until that point, the team of 1994 was still winning.

Jeff Brown held an ownership position in a Spokane software company working on artificial intelligence for classified government work. Scott Spink had degrees in engineering and business and was working on fuel cell research. Geoff Goss was an attorney. Marty Wall was an executive of a brewing company.

How did this group turn its Gonzaga basketball experience into such post-graduate success?

Brown offered a suggestion: "Must have been all of Fitz's positive reinforcement."

Band of Brothers

A decade after finishing up as a GU player, Jeff Brown said not a single day goes by that he doesn't receive a call or an email from a former teammate. Or, given the way these guys stay close, it's probably more accurate to contend that there is no such thing as a "former" teammate.

"Having transferred from Washington, I had two entirely different experiences," Brown said. "So I can say, yes, the experience at Gonzaga is unusual. You could see the best friendships in the world between guys like Geoff Goss and Jamie Dudley. They beat the hell out of each other in practice, and you know that a piece of them had to want the other to fail somewhat so they could get more playing time. But they are as good of friends as anybody can possibly be."

Getting His Just Desserts

Scott Spink thought Jeff Brown was being sort of a bully. It was in the cafeteria, and Brown had poached a piece of cake off the plate of teammate Jason Rubright, and wolfed down the purloined pastry with all-too-conspicuous gusto.

"It looked like some sort of chocolate cake with a white frosting," Brown said. But instead of going "yummmmm," Brown started saying something along the lines of, "aagggggg."

"My mouth started itching and swelling up," he said.

Brown is deathly allergic to legumes, beans and peanuts, etc. One tiny little goober can put him in the hospital, and an absence of attention to his reaction could cause death, or at least trigger derisive abuse from his teammates.

Jeff Brown shot his way to honors as the West Coast Conference Player of the Year (1994), and also was recognized as the nation's top scholar-athlete.

With tongue swelling and throat closing, Brown croaked: "What kind of cake was that?"

His friends reported, with some amusement: "Peanut butter."

"We had seen him take the cake off Jason's plate and his face turned a funny color and it looked like his head was swelling up," Spink said.

As was the way with this group, the immediate response to Brown's emergency was to suggest that he shouldn't have stolen the cake in the first place, and if he couldn't breathe, well, instant karma can be tough to swallow.

"Yeah, there's some truth to that, probably a lot of truth to that," Brown said of their unhurried attention.

He should have expected his teammates' cool reaction. "Very few of the guys understood how serious this was," Brown said. "When we used to fly, some of the knuckleheads used to throw peanuts in my direction to try to see if they could land them in my mouth."

The day of the cake incident, Brown ended up in Sacred Heart Medical Center's emergency room, finally able to breathe, but with a newfound respect for the sanctity of other people's desserts.

Busting Chops

Nothing was exempt from ridicule. Jeff Brown may have been dying from a severe allergic reaction, but some teammates were going to bust on him between his gasps. During games, make a mistake, somebody would chew on you. Any gathering of these verbal vipers, in fact, quickly made a Friars' Roast look like a Rotary breakfast.

"We always operated in a culture that would not allow you to take yourself too seriously," Brown said. "It was continuous joking, and also really laying into each other. People who don't know us would think we were awful to each other, but that was just the way we interacted."

Goss and Brown would go at it during games, too, with Brown recalling one game at Santa Clara in particular when Goss failed to take a hit to stop a two-on-one fast break.

"I said, 'Would you take a goddamned charge?' and he shot right back at me, 'Would you make a goddamned shot?' and Matt [Stanford] had to jump in and say, 'Would you both just shut the hell up?'"

The self-policing approach took place after the games, too, when the group would creatively and enthusiastically discover ways to replenish fluids.

"Let's just say that for us it was a work-hard, play-hard thing," Brown said. Weren't they noted for playing too hard? "I guess that's open to judgment, but by the time the season rolled around, we were pretty serious. And we held each other pretty accountable."

And the Oscar Goes to ...

... Marc Armstead. The Zags were locked in a close game at Loyola Marymount in 1993, the sort of game that is generally claimed by some measure of athletic heroics ... not theatrics.

"Something happened where Marc Armstead got fouled," Jeff Brown remembered. "Now, he's like Shaq at the free-throw line, terrible. But as he realizes he's going to get some free throws, he falls to the floor holding his back and wincing. I mean, he's in pain, literally laying on the floor."

Brown rushed to his aid. And when LMU coach John Olive started accusing Armstead of putting on an act to keep from having to go to the free-throw line, an indignant Brown got in his face and questioned his lack of sportsmanship and compassion ... in so many words.

"How dare he accuse him of faking it?" Brown asked. "Armstead hobbled off the floor with an ice pack on his back and John Rillie, a 90-percent free-throw shooter came on and made two free throws."

The next day as they studied videos of the game, Brown recalled, a wide shot showed some of the bench area as Rillie netted the free throw that gave GU the 65-64 victory.

"There was Armstead jumping up and down when that second free throw went in," Brown said. "He had miraculously recovered."

They're Just Good Friends

Jeff Brown conceded that his teammates kidded him about being coach Dan Fitzgerald's "Golden Boy." He has an example that shows his favored status.

"We were at Santa Clara in Jarrod Davis' senior year," Brown said. "That year, Fitz and Jarrod didn't really see eye to eye. Santa Clara had just scored and I had to take the ball out of the net and throw it to the point guard. I thought Jamie Dudley was covered, although he claims now that he was wide open. But I saw Jarrod running up the sideline over by our bench, and I decided to throw it to him."

But the instant Brown unleashed the pass, Davis turned and cut back up the floor. Brown's pass hit him on the back, ricocheted toward the bench, and nailed Fitzgerald in the head.

"I think, 'Oh, shit, I'm gonna get killed,'" Brown said. "But instead, Fitz yanked Jarrod and gave him hell."

Cold Shower

The Zags had won their 20th game in a season for the first time at the Division I level. It was merely two seasons after they had suffered through the dismal 1990 20-loss campaign.

Upon reaching the locker room after the 54-51 win over Santa Clara in the West Coast Conference Tournament, Jeff Brown, Eric Brady and Jarrod Davis decided that a festive way to mark the occasion would be to dump the cooler with ice water on head coach Dan Fitzgerald.

Teams do that to their coaches all the time, right? The coach laughs, they all hug. Good times.

"We were stoked, and we knew he was, too," Brown said. "So he comes in and we throw it on him."

About the time the first icy drop hit him, it started turning to steam, as Fitzgerald detonated.

"We thought he was going to kill us all," Brown said. "It went from this very joyous moment one second to, 'Uh-oh, we REALLY should not have done this.' Let's just say that he was NOT pleased."

Jarrod Davis (Zag, '92) was not only an All-West Coast Conference selection, but also an academic All-American.

Zag Evolution

Some players think the transfer of Jeff Brown from Washington to GU was a point when Zag fortunes turned steeply upward. "That, as much as anything, could have been the point when things got turned around," Scott Spink said. "Because he was awesome; he could score on anybody. He knew what his job was, and that was to score points."

Brown, though, believes that "very good coaching is the biggest part of it."

"Luck is a piece of it, but they've recruited the right kind of players and success with them breeds more success," Brown said. "You win more games, get more publicity, and the doors open to get better recruits. And when you have success with one approach, it tends to draw players who appreciate the same approach. In other words, selfish guys aren't drawn to Gonzaga. The atmosphere is ultra-competitive, and that's the kind of people who flourish there."

What results is a continuum of like-minded athletes through the years, each benefiting from the efforts of his predecessors, and likewise improving matters for future Zags.

"I know I had it easier than Ken Anderson, Hugh Hobus, Jim McPhee and Doug Spradley," Brown said. "And guys who came after me certainly play in nicer arenas. What happens is, I see a Blake Stepp or Casey Calvary or Richie Frahm, and there's an instant bond there. The crux of the program is the same; it's changed, but not dramatically, and so there's a bond there."

Goss Almost Tossed

Dan Fitzgerald calls time out. Gonzaga's down but has the ball.

He tells point guard Geoff Goss to dribble up, feed Jeff Brown inside, and the Zags get a win in their first game of the 1992 University of Alabama-Birmingham Classic.

"I dribbled up the side, Brown's man literally falls down and there's nobody within 10 feet of him," Goss recalled. "But for some reason I fired up a 22-footer from the corner, falling out of bounds, and it goes 15 feet over the rim. Fitz looked at me, kicked his chair, threw his pen about 30 rows into the stands and says to me, 'Goss, you are the worst point guard I've ever seen; you are done for good.'"

The Zags lost that one in double overtime, but rallied back the next night with a win over Alcorn State.

"So, we go have a few beers ... and I had a few too many," Goss said. "Marty Wall, my roommate, was supposed to wake me up, but he didn't. So everybody is out there at 6 a.m. wearing their ties and ready to fly. I show up in my Nike sweats. I almost got cut on the spot. It took me about another year and a half to get back on his good side."

Running Bare

A group of Zags watched the National League Championship Series of 1992 with interest. The Pittsburgh Pirates held a lead over the Atlanta Braves in Game 7, and Geoff Goss impetuously offered a wager on the outcome.

"I told the guys that if the Braves came back to win this, I'd do a dead sprint from there to the library naked," Goss said. "I'll never forget Francisco Cabrera got this hit in the bottom of the ninth and the Braves ended up winning and going to the World Series. My first thought was, 'Holy shit, what now?' I put on a Gonzaga stocking cap and shoes and take off. It's about four or five blocks, and those guys trailed me the whole way screaming my name so people would be sure to look."

It was dusk, and the campus was crowded. So, this was one fast break that Goss regretted.

"It was very, very unattractive," he said.

Geoff Goss: Being a Zag

"I think the common thread throughout is that you've got guys who are 1) intelligent, 2) highly competitive, and, 3) want to get better and are willing to do what it takes to do so.

"There have been a bunch of solid, hard-working and ambitious types playing there. We pushed each other; you didn't want to be the one who messed up, in school, or drinking beers, or on the court. Everybody would jump your ass, and you had to get better and have a pretty strong will.

"Now, they're at a point where they can get guys with those qualities who have some huge talent, too. We take pride in that, absolutely. It's like a big, close-knit fraternity."

A Rodent's Retort

Frankly, Geoff Goss didn't care for his nickname: The Gerbil.

It was a function of his hyperactivity, especially in his early years at Gonzaga. When Jeff Brown would taunt him, Goss responded by labeling him: "First-team All-Sizzler."

The volleying continues long after the playing days.

"I saw him recently," Goss said. "And I told him he looked like that Jared guy BEFORE he started eating at Subway."

Hide the Women and Children

One practice into Geoff Goss's career at Gonzaga, head coach Dan Fitzgerald turned to assistant Dan Monson with a line Monson has never forgotten.

"He said, 'If we're gonna coach that guy, we're gonna need helmets and shoulder pads for protection because that ball is flying everywhere,'" Monson said. "Goss was a real character because he had so much energy and was so hyper. His roommate his freshman year [Scott Spink] kept complaining to us that Goss would be over in his bunk bouncing the ball off the wall at two in the morning."

According to Monson, Fitzgerald would find a guy, frequently his point guard, and coach through him. For several years, that was Goss. But the guy never capitulated.

"What was so impressive about Goss," Monson said. "Was that he took it and took it and never was broken by it. I think that's what helped him become such a good player."

Members of the successful '94 Zag team, reconvening for a 10-year reunion in 2004, include (left to right): John Nemeth, Scott Morgan, Scott Spink, Matt Stanford, Jon Kinloch, Geoff Goss and Jeff Brown.

Another Vote for the '94 Zags

Alumni director Marty Pujolar has traveled with the basketball team since 1980, and has seen enough to fill his own lengthy tome.

But while other Gonzaga teams have had more success, he still relishes the memories of the classic '94 Zag team with Geoff Goss, Jeff Brown, Matt Stanford, etc.

"That group was not only a really good basketball team, but those guys were the most fun," Pujolar said. "They were smart, they could perform on the court, perform in the classroom, and they were absolutely the most fun guys to be around."

Somehow, they balanced competitiveness with a rational perspective. Or at least the capacity to drown their dismay after losses.

"These guys didn't take it so seriously," Pujolar said. "The recent groups are so stoic. They win a big game, they go back to their rooms and study or play video games. These guys went out and celebrated. They knew where the line was, though, and they looked out for each other. You know what, a lot of times I'd go with them. They were a lot of fun and they probably just looked at me as a guy who didn't grow up and just wanted to have a good time, too."

Contemporary teams are more successful, and also more orderly, Pujolar noted.

"It seems a little more methodical," he said. "It used to be that we'd go out on the floor and have no idea what was going to happen. In the roller coaster of Gonzaga basketball I've seen, I'd say that there used to be more losses, but I'm not going to say it was any less fun. We had a lot of great kids and coaches."

Zag Quip

Some of the old Zags from the early 1990s have asked coach Mark Few if he thought that their affinity for late-night "fellowship" conspired to make them somewhat less successful than the later GU teams that attained national prominence.

Few has a cutting response: "I tell them, 'No, you guys just weren't as good as the new guys.'"

CHAPTER TEN

Mons, Billy and More

Party of Three

In what might have worked as the set-up for a sitcom on the Fox Network, coaches Dan Monson, Mark Few and Bill Grier lived together for several years in a home on Wiscomb Street on the north side of Spokane.

It was Monson's house; Few paid rent, and Grier offered whatever services he could and chipped in whenever possible since he was, at the time, the lowly restricted-earnings coach on the staff.

Their colleagues at other universities predicted disaster; the three would be committing assault and battery on each other's person before the first season was finished. But it worked without bloodshed.

"We never got tired of each other," said Monson, the landlord. "We're different people at work than we were at home, and we had so much in common, if somebody wanted to play tennis, it seemed like all three of us did, or go golfing or fishing. We never had any troubles."

"We just had a lot of fun together," Grier said. "People in our profession couldn't believe we could do it and make it work. Coaches spend so much time together in practice and on the road,

*Coach Dan Monson led the Zags to the 1999 NCAA Elite Eight and
a narrow loss to eventual champion Connecticut.*

to live together too seemed like a lot. But we were literally like a band of brothers. Mark and I had been close in college, and we had that same closeness with Dan."

No battles?

"Oh, there were times when we bickered and argued," Grier said. "Mostly it was about recruits, who we needed and who we wanted. It's also a pretty competitive group of guys. We'd golf or play hoops at noon, and the competitive side came out of all of us. Also in lawn darts ... we were big lawn-darts guys."

Monson was an absentee landlord much of the time as he and Few were often on the road scouting or recruiting.

"Every day that was open, we were out on the road," Few said. "So Dan and I were gone a lot. But we played a lot of golf, too. People kept saying it would be tough to do, work together and live together, but it never seemed that way. We just had a great time and a lot of fun."

Poverty Flats

Bill Grier laughs when he recalls the name of his position: Restricted-earnings coach.

"Yeah," he said. "It was VERY restricted."

Until a class-action lawsuit did away with the practice, and earned the oppressed minority a hefty check for wages owed, universities were able to indenture a third basketball coach for the annual stipend of $5,000. (Job description: All the menial tasks you can tolerate for about $100 a week).

When Dan Monson offered to let him bunk in with the guys on Wiscomb Street, it saved Grier considerable grief.

"Dan was so great," Grier said. "He told me I could just pay him whatever I could and we'd just figure it out and not worry about it. He really, really helped me out."

Grier was determined to earn his keep. Aside from learning his craft as a coach in what amounts to a glorified apprenticeship, he mowed the lawn and cleaned the house. "Some nights, Dan would say, 'I'll buy some food, you cook.'"

Although this didn't appear on his coaching resume, Grier had useful experience to draw upon. His father used to own a dinner house, and in the summers, Grier worked in the kitchen at the stove.

As his roommates discovered, he also worked well in the basement.

Billy's Best Moves

The curious courting rituals of college basketball coaches have never been a topic studied by anthropologists. But Dan Monson and Mark Few couldn't help but make note of Bill Grier's romantic tendencies.

"At one point, all of us were fairly single," Mark Few said of the three coaches/roomies. "And then I was attached and the two of them were single. One or two of those summers, Billy was on quite a roll, so that was interesting."

Interesting? Meaning that Few and Monson took amusement from Grier's dating regimen?

"Oh, yeah," Few said. "Totally."

"He was quite routine-oriented," Few said of Grier. "He had this garden he was growing, and he'd take vegetables out of the garden, then he'd prepare dinner for the date. At the time, he was the guy who put together our highlight videos, so, after dinner, he'd take her downstairs into what we called The Bermuda Triangle—our big sectional sofa—and pretty soon you'd hear the music from the video playing."

Few and Monson upstairs acted responsibly, of course. "We'd just start laughing," Few said. "It was like clockwork: Come in, go the garden, harvest the vegetables, make some dinner, highlight film ... off he goes. I have to say he had a pretty good run there, very impressive."

Free Billy

Worries over enrollment and budgetary shortfalls caused the Gonzaga administration to consider taking serious measures toward economizing in the summer of 1998. In a sit-down of department heads, tough questions were asked, and some started looking around for positions to eliminate.

Athletic director Mike Roth found himself fending off inquiries why the men's basketball program needed three full-time coaches. At the time, Dan Monson was head coach, with Mark Few the top assistant and Bill Grier the third coach, who was unknowingly facing treacherously impermanent employment status.

"These were really tough times, and people lost their jobs," Roth said. "But we fought them off."

Before that school year had finished, the Zags had gone to the NCAA West Regional in Seattle and defeated Minnesota and Stanford on their way to an Elite Eight defeat against Connecticut.

"I later went back to [the administrators] and pointed out to them that the coach who did the great job of scouting and preparing the team for the win over Stanford was Billy Grier," Roth said. "I was able to show them that was exactly the reason we needed that guy."

Was the message received?

"It was the last time anybody ever asked why we needed three coaches," Roth said.

The attendance woes that led to the campus-wide belt-tightening, meanwhile, disappeared as the basketball success continued.

"Freshman enrollment at the time was about 400 and change, and it's more than doubled to over 900 and change," Roth said. "It's gotten to where we had to put a cap on it."

That's a development that more than adequately paid for Grier's salary over that span.

Unlucky Break

Dan Fitzgerald expected full-service assistants, sometimes asking them to fill in during drills that required another player. One year, when the redshirts were home on Christmas break, Fitzgerald forced Bill Grier into action.

"The first possession I'm out there, I got up to guard Jamie Dudley," Grier said. "I was not nearly up to the level of those guys, aside from not being in good enough shape. But these guys go hard, so I wanted to do my best. The very first possession, I get up close to Dudley and he leans into me and catches my nose flush with the side of his head. I hear this crunch and my nose goes over to the side of my face."

Coach Jerry Krause broke out in uncontrollable laughter, thinking Grier was kidding.

How did Fitz respond?

"He didn't say anything," Grier said. "He was probably pissed he couldn't run the drill any more."

Hands-on Coaching

Looking at the GU coaching staff caused Ryan Floyd to draw an interesting conclusion: "This must be the shortest squad of coaches in the country."

Mark Few, Billy Grier and Leon Rice were not physically imposing, but commanded respect.

"It's so obvious they understand the game so well," Floyd said. "They recruit high-quality guys and they know who is going to fit into the system and who is going to fit in with the team."

But their input was not solely administrative or strategic, Floyd discovered when he found himself in a drill in which Grier was competing.

"Billy stepped in and just absolutely kicked my ass," Floyd said. "He's a scrappy little sucker and he drove me nuts. He'd be hustling and setting back picks and getting all over you. I came in as a freshman walk-on trying to make an impression, and to discover that the coach can kick your ass is a real humbling experience."

No Pink Slip

The joke around the office was that head coach Dan Fitzgerald would fire his assistants so regularly during games that they'd have to convene at night just to see who was still employed. Dan Monson, though, said it only happened once to him.

"He said that to me once during a game," Monson said. "I had heard he had done that in the past in the heat of a game. I went into his office the next morning and said that I had a lot of respect for him and I loved working for him, and he has the right to fire me whenever he wants. But I told him he wasn't going to do it during a game again. I told him it was his prerogative, but if he was going to do it, it was going to be just the two of us in his office. I loved working for him and we had a huge mutual respect and still do."

It's just always good to know you're going to be employed until the final buzzer.

Monson's Miracle Cure

The Gonzaga basketball team started out winless in its first six West Coast Conference games in 1995. The team was coming off a season when it advanced to the second round of the NIT, and a pre-conference campaign when it lost only once in 12 contests.

So the winless start in conference mystified the coaches. Hoping to snap the sorry streak, assistant coach Dan Monson called the team into a circle at the start of one practice and, in the spirit of a television evangelist "curing" them by placing his hand on their foreheads and causing them to collapse, Monson infused them with faith.

"He had found this sign behind the bleachers that had been used for something else and it said, 'I Believe,'" manager Drew Dannels said. "He had them read the sign and look into everybody's eyes and say it like they meant it. If they didn't say it with enough meaning, he made them say it until it sounded real. I think it really got through to them what they had to do."

The effect of Brother Monson's Revival? The Zags went 7-1 the remainder of the conference season, rolled through the WCC Tournament and advanced to the NCAA Tournament for the first time in school history.

"As I look back, it's clear in my head that this was one time when a coach stepped up and was able to show them that they just needed to regain their confidence," Dannels said. "They just need to believe they could play as well as they could."

Moment of Truth

If asked to identify one specific fulcrum point upon which the GU program turned steeply upward, some recalled a practice early in the 1997-98 season when new coach Dan Monson issued an unmistakable mandate to his team.

"We had one practice early when they weren't going very hard," Bill Grier remembered. "Dan blew up and kicked them out of practice; kicked them off the court. He followed them into the locker room and just laid into them like you wouldn't believe."

Monson challenged them as players and as men and as Zags. He demanded accountability to each other and to themselves. The kind of effort he'd seen, he stressed—at forceful decibels—would not be tolerated.

"This was a year of transition," Grier said. "It was Dan's first year and the players may have been testing him, and testing the young staff. But they didn't have any problems understanding his point. And from that moment, they really bought into it."

In Defeat, Promise

Nice scheduling. Dan Monson opened his second season as GU head coach, in the late fall of 1998, against Kansas AT Kansas.

"At the time, they had something like a 40-game home win streak going," Monson recalled.

A visiting team with limited cachet such as Gonzaga has a tough time getting calls at a place like Kansas, but the Zags led most of the game before falling down the stretch. As he approached the locker room, Monson started going through his possible postgame comments to the team. He couldn't be too hard on them, he reasoned, because nobody came to Kansas and won at the time.

"But I walked into that locker room and it was a shambles," Monson said. "I had to get on them about it. But I loved that they were so upset about it. They weren't blaming the officials or anything; they were blaming themselves that they didn't win. They were really mad about not winning that game. Here I was, trying to find excuses to make it not seem so bad to them, but I realized they were right. They raised my expectations. I needed to be mad, too. They're the ones who taught me that it was unacceptable for us to lose, no matter who it was against or where it was played. I knew right then that was going to be a fun group to coach."

He had fun ... all the way to the West Regional finals.

Persistent Gophers

Well-schooled, prepared, inspired and motivated, the Zags tore through the 1999 NCAA Tournament bracket in an unexpected dash that not only highlighted the program, but also cast a spotlight on head coach Dan Monson.

He'd been a head coach for only two seasons, but to get Gonzaga within a last-minute loss of the Final Four was to stamp him as a sizzling commodity in the ever-volatile coaching market.

Schools had flashed cash at him, but nothing that loosed his moorings. Until Minnesota called. Only a few months earlier, Monson had led the heavy underdog Zags to a win over the Golden Gophers in the first round of the NCAA Tournament. Minnesota administrators not only noticed how well coached the Zags were, but also how the group of student-athletes provided such a stark contrast to their own team, which was beset by academic scandal.

Monson, they reasoned, was the man to lead the team, and also to cleanse the tainted image. And they would not relent.

"I didn't want to be one of those coaches chasing the almighty dollar," Monson said. "You can't just take a job solely for money. I took pride in the idea that I was at Gonzaga for the right reasons. And it wasn't a good time in my life to change. I was engaged to be married, and I had just come back from coaching USA Basketball and I hadn't had time to be with my team and enjoy that Elite Eight run we had accomplished."

So, although the offer was for a significant raise, he told Minnesota "no."

But they persisted. They upped the ante again. Monson, once again, said no. Even with the money, Minnesota would be too far away from his family. That was too important to him.

"They said, well, we'll give you an account you can use to fly your family back and forth to games," Monson said. "I wasn't going to leave to take just any job, and it had to be a special situation."

Addressing the family issue convinced Monson that Minnesota was serious about what it wanted in its basketball program, and that it was a place he would feel welcomed and wanted.

And the raise? From $100,000 a year to $7 million over 10 years. It would take him 70 years of coaching at his current rate to make that money at GU.

Because previous coach Clem Haskins had overseen a program that was about to land on serious probation for academic misdeeds, the administration at Minnesota was in no position to place immediate win-loss demands on the new coach.

"This job looked like they were going to give me time to do it my way, to try to get the good student-athletes," Monson said. "I decided that if I ever wanted to try coaching at another level, this would be the best case because they really wanted me and showed they'd do whatever it took to get me there."

Good-Bye, Buddy

The money, the challenge of stepping up, the uncertainty, at the time, whether Gonzaga could sustain its competitive momentum ... Dan Monson battled through wavering evaluations of all those factors.

It was a time of soul searching for him. And for his friends and colleagues, it was hardly easier. The decision didn't entirely catch his staff offguard, as Monson had been wooed before. But this was not a capricious career move plotted by a serial stair-stepping coach. And the entire staff was deeply affected.

"It was just the total gamut of every emotion you could have," Mark Few said. "There was excitement about what was going to happen next, there was some obvious apprehension about what was going on with me, and there was a definite, definite sadness over losing a really, really close friend you'd worked beside for 10 years. That was really hard."

From a practical standpoint, the change was barely noticeable, seeing that one of Monson's best qualities was his capacity to delegate. He had always told Few that he considered them "co-coaches."

"He was never threatened by that; he delegated so well, and it's an approach I have tried to take, too," Few said. "Dan was a great communicator with the players. He wouldn't beat around the bush with guys, they always knew right where they stood. He was always very perceptive, and he'd tell guys, 'This is where you are and this is where I think you need to be.' Players really appreciated that."

Who Gets Custody of Billy?

Mark Few saw Dan Monson struggle with a huge career decision, and then dealt with the same hand wringing with his other friend, Bill Grier. If he stayed with Few at Gonzaga, Grier would move over a seat and become the top assistant and heir apparent in the event of

*Coach Bill Grier was an important component of GU success while
assisting Dan Fitzgerald, Dan Monson and Mark Few.*

Few's departure. If he went with Monson to Minnesota, well, it was the Big 10 Conference, where there's a lot of money getting tossed around. For a guy who had been the restricted-earnings coach at GU, raking in a cool five grand a year, the chance to rocket up a few tax brackets had to hold some allure.

"A tough part of this was, what are we going to do with Billy?" Few said. "Is he staying or is he going?"

Grier was not wishboned by a battle of bids, or asked to be the fraying rope in a tug of war between friends. He was merely offered options.

"We both just talked to him and told him what the deal was," Few said. "I think it was a hard decision for him. He would get compensated a lot more money at Minnesota and he had to look at that, of course. But he also knew we really had something pretty special that was building here, and he knew he was in a large part responsible for that, and it was something to feel very good about."

The shuffle of old roommates and friends left Monson on his way to Minnesota, Few stepping up to the head coach's chair, and Grier staying in Spokane alongside Few.

Neener, Neener, Neener

Jerry Krause coached 17 seasons at Eastern Washington University. When he was fired with several games remaining in the 1983 season, GU coach Dan Fitzgerald called him immediately and offered him a job.

Fitzgerald respected the work Krause had done at Eastern and was upset with the way the long-time Eagle coach had been treated by his administration. In a delicious bit of timing that delighted Fitzgerald, Gonzaga was scheduled to play host to EWU only days after Krause was fired.

"I don't care what profession you're in, you never think you're going to be the one to get fired," Krause said. "It's a shock to you; it's one of those defining moments in your life, and how you respond to it is the story."

How Fitzgerald responded was the REAL story.

"He was amazing," Krause said. "When Eastern came over to play Gonzaga, Fitz had a special award made up for me in honor of my 'Special Contributions to Basketball in the Region' and they had a ceremony for me at halftime of the game while all the EWU administrators were in the stands squirming. It was great. It was really great."

Taking Charge

Jerry Krause coached basketball in the Inland Empire since shortly after they replaced the peach baskets on each end of the court. So he's a credible source for tracking the roots of Gonzaga's image.

"You have to give [coach Dan Fitzgerald] credit for establishing the identity for the Gonzaga program," Krause said. "He brought the blue-collar work ethic: We're going to be tougher than anybody we play. When you build on that identity, that we're going to rebound and play defense and take charges and play smart, then that's the kind of players you get. And it's okay to do that with lesser talented people if they're dedicated enough."

To a point.

"What Dan [Monson] and Mark [Few] brought to the program was the recruiting," Krause said. "They had a vision that if they got good players who fit the foundation, the Gonzaga identity, then they could compete against anybody. They sold the kids on that vision, and that's how they got some of those players."

The earliest seeds of this attitude, Krause said, were sown even before Fitzgerald, by another San Francisco-area product, coach Bud Presley, who assisted head coach Hank Anderson.

"Bud was really the blue-collar guy; he set a standard even for guys like Fitz," Krause said. "He used to start practice every year with his team by taking seven charges himself. He'd be screaming, 'Come on, come on, hit me, hit me, take me down.'"

And they did.

"He went down for the count one time," Krause said. "With cracked ribs."

CHAPTER ELEVEN

Mighty Casey

The Ogre

The body posture was fearsome enough, and there was an attitude that exuded toughness. But with Casey Calvary, the most frightening thing may have been the slightly psychotic gaze. All too often for opponents' tastes, he flashed those intense eyes that could focus as fiercely as that magician who can bend spoons with just his telekinetic stare.

He even scared the staff a little.

"He was probably the all-time worst guy to have around when you brought a recruit onto campus," Mark Few said of Calvary. "He had no understanding at all of whether this kid was a little under-developed but had great potential. There was never any political correctness about him. He would tell the kid exactly what he thought of him. You'd just be cringing that he would say something to him."

Of course, when the players actually showed up on campus, Calvary ceased being so sensitive.

"For an entire year, the freshmen would operate in fear of just going to practice," Few said. "But he's part of what made our team so tough and competitive. He simply did not tolerate weakness, it bothered him. He would seek it out and do everything he could to squash it."

Coach Billy Grier called Calvary "The Ogre." In the most respectful of ways, of course.

"He was by far the most stubborn guy we've ever had," Grier said. "But his stubbornness was what made him such a good competitor on the floor. He gave off that don't-mess-with-me aura and he gets these crazy eyes that look right into you."

The attitude was contagious, spreading down through the ranks as new players were annually added and indoctrinated.

"Some of those young big guys hated going to practice against him every day," Few said. "When Cory Violette got here, Casey just beat the snot out of him every day. But if you ask Cory about it, that really helped him get motivated."

Yeah, blood and bruises and baleful glares can do that.

Ogre with a Cause

He'll admit it, Casey Calvary had an attitude. Sometimes he was abrasive or curt or threatening. But in a good way.

"We had guys who liked to compete, and, sure, I'm a person who doesn't like to lose or get scored on," Calvary said. "And if those are morning practices, yeah, I would be cranky and pissy and it was easy to get irritated. But I never got in a fight with a teammate; your teammates are the guys you go to war with."

Verbal abuse was another matter, of course.

"Certainly, I always pitched a lot of shit at the freshmen and young guys; that's what seniors do. But you also need to maintain the persona of a good leader so that when they get into the game, they have confidence, they know you're not afraid and they shouldn't be, either."

On the court, in the face of opponents, Calvary's aspect and attitude was productively fearsome; guards paid heed to his presence and stayed outside glowering radius.

"Even if you don't block a shot, if you've got them thinking about what you're going to do when they come in the key, that can be a factor," he said. "If you can get them a little afraid or a little off balance, it affects their confidence."

Calvary Rides to Rescue

The signing of point guard Matt Santangelo a year earlier had been an enormous boost to the Zags, but when Dan Monson looks back, the conscription of Casey Calvary out of Tacoma's Bellarmine Prep went a long way to securing the future of GU hoops.

"It was so tough the year that Fitz decided to step down because I wasn't going to be the head coach for another year," Monson said. "In hindsight, that was probably a negative thing to do. We thought it was an honest way to let the kids know who they're going to be playing for and what direction the program was going. But we got absolutely crucified by other schools saying, 'He's never been a head coach before, how do you know what his style of play will be?'

"It was so hard and so stressful trying to get those kids to believe," Monson said. "We had to try to tell them what we thought was going to happen, and it was a huge leap of faith for them to go along with it."

Calvary had visited GU and liked it, but he also had a trip scheduled to Colorado State which, at the time, was probably considered a higher profile program.

"Casey called me when I was at the golf tournament for the Bulldog Club," Monson said. "And when he told me, 'I want to play for you, Coach,' that was one I'll never forget. He was the first one to take that leap of faith that I was going to be a coach he'd like to play for."

The Basket Hanger

The picture appeared so often in newspapers that it almost came to symbolize Gonzaga basketball: Casey Calvary looking as if he'd just executed a pull-up on the rim, legs tucked up to make him appear even more disrespectful of gravity, face clenched into something that seemed to say "take that, net." Usually, somewhere near the bottom of the frame was a cowering opponent just trying to avoid potential backboard shrapnel. It was Calvary in his customary post-dunk posture, buried up to his armpits in the hoop.

Casey Calvary's dunks only counted two points, but some were so dramatic that teammates claimed they could change the course of the game.
Tom Hauck/Getty Images

There was no finesse to this move. It is nothing but lift and thrust, mass and velocity. And it was at once frightful and entertaining to behold.

And from among the collection of Calvary's highlight dunks, a favorite emerges because of its context. "We were playing Cincinnati, and they may have been No. 1 in the country at that time, with Kenyon Martin getting a lot of publicity as a national Player-of-the-Year candidate," Few said. "Casey came at him with one of the most vicious dunks I've ever seen."

As Few recalled, Calvary spotted Martin down near the basket, and powered up the lane straight at him. Martin took the challenge and the two collided as if engaged in a Medieval joust.

"Martin actually took a swing at him, hitting Casey under the eye, but Casey just flew right through him," Few said. "Casey needed four or five stitches to close the cut, but he jammed on him so hard it was unbelievable."

And then?

"Casey," Few said, "just stared right through him."

Blood and Dunks

Calvary still has the scar below his left eye from the encounter with Kenyon Martin. But whereas the pain subsided, the good memories remain.

"I back-cut my guy and got a bounce pass from Mattie [Santangelo]," Calvary said. "Kenyon was guarding another guy in the post and I didn't even see him coming at me. I went up and he came after me. I think he was trying to volleyball punch it out of there to keep from getting dunked on."

Calvary not only got the basket, but also was sent to the line for a free throw. Instead of shooting, though, he had to be taken out because of the bleeding.

"He was such a great player and an intimidating force on the basketball court that dunking on him is definitely a highlight I keep in my mind."

And also under his left eye.

Casey Calvary: Being a Zag

While some have pinpointed the acquisition and development of Casey Calvary as a force behind Gonzaga's run of success, Calvary points elsewhere.

"It begins and ends with the coaching staff," he said. "The changes they implemented in going from the Flex offense to the Motion, the green light they gave us, them having the confidence in us. They have found a certain mold for what makes a good Zag. And guys who don't fit the mold either don't come or don't stay.

"It's not always the best players, not always the local players, but guys who work hard, who put the team first, who enjoy doing what we do on the court, and who EXPECT to win. The jersey doesn't win games for you, but when you put it on, it sure makes you angry with yourself if you lose. The staff has done an incredible job of finding guys who will buy into all that."

The Late Dan Monson

Casey Calvary laughs now when thinking how worried Gonzaga coaches Dan Monson and Mark Few were over getting caught in traffic and being tardy for their appointed home visit with him.

"If they had known my dad like they do now, they'd have known they had nothing to fear," Calvary said. "He was a military guy, and he's very punctual, but he's also very laid back and a very friendly man. My dad had some questions for them just in terms of where I was going to spend the next four or five years of my life."

Apparently relieved that the elder Calvary didn't make them pull KP duty, the young Zag coaches made their best pitch. And Calvary liked what he heard.

"It was kind of trial by fire for those guys; Mons hadn't been a head coach and he hadn't proven himself, so it left them trying to sell what they could grow into rather than what they actually were. That's a difficult thing to do, but they did a good job."

The home visit wasn't the clincher for Calvary, though. The players at the school at the time did the best job of luring him to Spokane.

"When I got there and talked to everybody on campus, you could tell they took basketball seriously, they played hard, and it was close enough that my parents could come to the games," Calvary said. "That's what really made everything fall into place."

Zag Quip

It was the spring of 1999 and guard Matt Santangelo was asked about teammate Casey Calvary, GU's search-and-destroy post man.

"You can't even explain his desire and his competitiveness," Santangelo said. "People say dunks are only worth two points, but he can sometimes change the whole tempo of the game, the whole feeling of the game with one dunk."

CHAPTER TWELVE

Fitz

In This Corner ... Dan Fitzgerald

Idaho State played its basketball games in a multipurpose domed football stadium. And the crowd brought a correspondingly rowdy football attitude to the games.

In December 1991, the Zags broke open a close game in the final couple minutes, and the Bengal fans started getting hostile.

Bill Grier, the restricted-earnings coach at the time, was included in the traveling party only because Zag Marty Wall overslept and was left home. So Grier had a ringside seat to watch the postgame bout.

"The fans were giving Mark [Few] a hard time about his tie and they were calling Dan [Monson] 'Coach Rogaine,'" Grier said. "Right at the end of the game, somebody started throwing things out of the stands and a coin or something hit Fitz."

Uh-oh. Stand back. Fitzgerald, who grew up boxing in the parks of San Francisco, wouldn't stand for this.

"He turned around and pointed at the guy," Grier said. "He yelled, 'You, bring it down here, right here, right now.'"

Zag Eric Brady saw the escalating hostilities and knew his coach was not one to back down, so he tossed a towel around Fitzgerald's neck and took him by the shoulders and led him—like a boxer leaving the ring—off the floor. The players almost collapsed from the sight.

"We were dressing in this football locker room," Grier said. "And by the time we got in there, Brady and Jeff Brown had put on helmets and shoulder pads and were running into each other ... just making fun of the whole situation."

Fitzgerald didn't mind if the players sensed in him a tough-guy persona.

"The guys used to love it," Grier said. "When Fitz would tell them the stories about growing up in the park, getting a six pack of beer and a pack of cigarettes and going down to the park to beat the crap out of each other just for something to do."

Brown remembered Fitzgerald making his challenge to the coin-tossing fan. It was unruly to a dangerous degree, he said.

"At a timeout one time, some Idaho State fan took off his cowboy hat and put it on my head," Brown said. "When that thing was over, there was no security and we had to make our way up the ramp with no crowd control. Fitz was slamming into people and we're zig-zagging through the crowd. It was like a scene from *Slapshot*."

What Brown Can't Do for You

Dan Fitzgerald was not one to pass on the opportunity to get in a barb about a coaching miscue if the situation presented itself.

"The first Division I game I scouted was against Portland," Bill Grier said. "They had a big guy named Stuckey who didn't seem to play very well away from the basket, never shot the jumper. One of the things I wrote in my report was that he was a guy we didn't have to guard away from the basket."

Center Jeff Brown, a diligent student of the scouting reports, took the advice literally, and when Stuckey broke out to the wing to take a pass, Brown merely stayed beneath the basket.

"Stuckey got the ball at the elbow with nobody near him," Grier recalled. "He licked his finger, tested the wind, and threw in a jump shot."

Fitzgerald walked past Grier at that moment and nailed him with: "You really missed on that guy."

"I was like, 'Yeah, but Brown doesn't have to turn and run away from him, either,'" Grier said. "Here I am, two minutes into the first game I scouted, and the head coach is on me."

Thanks, Fitz

Dan Fitzgerald didn't get the golden-watch send-off from Gonzaga, but old players still appreciate his efforts.

"Fitz was a great practice coach," Jarrod Davis said. "He motivated kind of through fear. The [coaches who followed] took it to the point where they convinced the players that they were as good as any team in the country; they instilled that. And it took them a while to get those players in there. That's why Gonzaga basketball is where it is. But I don't think Dan Fitzgerald gets the credit he deserves."

Fitz, Davis acknowledged, was "very hard to play for."

But the assistants he hired might never have gotten their start in college basketball if not for Fitzgerald, Davis said. "They are really good and they worked their tails off, and Fitz had to be hard to work for, but he gave them their shot. And if you look at the players we had, Geoff Goss walked on, Matt Stanford walked on, Eric Brady was a transfer, Jeff Brown was a transfer, I got a partial scholarship. Fitz gave us all our chances; he took a leap of faith with a lot of us, and he deserves a lot of gratitude from a lot of people."

Free Delivery

Coach Dan Fitzgerald, a man given to dramatic personal expression, stormed into the locker room after one game, grabbed the familiar flat box holding the customary postgame pizza, and let it fly like a big, square Frisbee.

"It was when Mark Spink was a freshman," manager Drew Dannels recalled. "Fitz was so pissed; he fired this thing and the box opened up in the air and pizza went flying everywhere. I looked over in the corner and there was Mark Spink with this huge chunk of cheese hanging off his head. It was hilarious."

But nobody in the room dared laugh.

"What's funny is we actually won that game," said Mark Spink, a redshirt freshman at the time. "I hadn't even played in that game. I was sitting next to Bakari Hendrix and Fitz picked up five or six of these pizzas. One of them headed right at Bakari, who was quick enough to get his hands up and block it so it wasn't a direct hit. But that had the effect of opening the pizza box and deflecting pizza all over me. So, I got the splatter effect from a ricochet shot."

Dueling Epitaphs

Geoff Goss's best Dan Fitzgerald line?

"He used to say that on his tombstone it would read: 'Goss ... Minus-5 Years'."

Goss countered that his might be inscribed: "I Played for Fitz ... Minus-15 Years."

Do Your Homework

Guard John Rillie recalls one game when Fitzgerald emphatically made a point.

"One night redshirt Keith Kincaid saw Fitz's temper," Rillie said. "As part of our pregame routine, he would go through the scouting report and randomly select a player to give a report on his man. You had to give a pretty astute answer or be very creative. Fitz called on Keith, and he was young and not really prepared. He looked at Fitz, gave him a laugh, and Fitz told him on the spot to get dressed and go home and study the report. See you later.

"So he could intimidate you," Rillie said. "But you knew he had a very good heart and a real soft spot for all the players."

Fitzism

Billy Grier, recalling Dan Fitzgerald's description of the ideal graduate assistant coach: "He always said he was looking for a Mormon with a motor home ... so he could be the designated driver for the whole staff."

Loose Leash

When Ken Anderson (Zag, '81) looks back, he wonders where the GU program might have gone if Dan Fitzgerald hadn't stepped down as coach and into the athletic director's role the first time, in the 1981-1985 span.

"I think that was the worst thing that could have happened to the program," Anderson said. "For whatever reason, we seemed to lose momentum. I think if Fitz had stayed on, we would have gone places sooner."

What Anderson liked was that Fitzgerald did not see himself as watchdog or armed guard.

"He let us do our thing," Anderson said. "And we were successful; all four of our seniors my year graduated and two of us got PhDs. I've been the faculty rep a long time and I've seen a lot of what's gone on. The thing about Fitz was that he was tough, and he wouldn't back down. But he let us do our thing and it really worked for our group."

The Zags were a reflection of their coach back then, Anderson said, tough, aggressive, fearless, entirely willing to be motivated by a chip on their shoulder, and in possession of a passion for basketball.

"It didn't matter what Fitz would be doing, whether you believed him or not, you always respected the passion he brought to it," Anderson said. "Whether he was building you up or throwing garbage cans around in a fit, he did it with passion. He'd tell you a story and you'd think, 'hmm, he's full of crap,' but it would be damned entertaining."

Gonzaga Lockout

Seismic readings suggested that Mount Fitzgerald would erupt at halftime. Drexel had been abusing the Zags like rental cars for the first 20 minutes of the Shootout Spokane game at The Kennel in December 1992.

Drexel, for heaven's sakes. Fitzgerald would have none of this.

Gonzaga had just gone to the new touch-pad locks with numerical codes on their locker rooms. When Dan Fitzgerald reached the locker room at half, his entrance was, let's say, forceful. He blasted his way into the locker room, issued some high-decibel "coaching," and stormed out, leaving the stunned players inside. When the door closed, it became evident that his NYPD method of opening it had broken the electronic lock.

Nobody could get in; the players couldn't get out.

Mike Roth, then director of facilities, not only had to call a locksmith to come over, he had to deal with the rantings of an irate and paranoid Drexel coach, who was certain this was just a ploy to extend halftime and cool off his team.

On the inside, as the story goes, Zag Marc Armstead got creative. Supposedly, he pulled some tweezers and medical tools out of trainer Steve DeLong's kit, disassembled the plate on the inside of the lock, and disarmed it ... freeing the Zags.

Whether inspired by Fitzgerald's outburst, or just grateful to be paroled from their smelly prison, the Zags then disposed of Drexel, 91-78.

Fitzism

When asked to scroll through his memory of hundreds of Dan Fitzgerald comments, Ken Anderson came up with one of his favorites.

"We drove past a poor homeless guy one time and Fitz says: 'Hey, that's the last coach who didn't win 20 games at Gonzaga.'"

*Dan Fitzgerald coached a lot of nailbiters as the
Gonzaga program was developing.*

Bench Warrior

Until he figured out a defense mechanism, trainer Steve DeLong took a beating. Sitting next to Dan Fitzgerald took its toll. The wild Irishman with a hair-trigger would come flying off the bench as if shot by a catapult, arms flying, veins bulging.

"He was a big man and tough," DeLong said. "He'd start flying around and he could really hurt you if you didn't protect yourself."

DeLong's tactics? "I started getting an assistant to sit next to Fitz to provide a buffer zone."

Even one seat removed from the danger radius of the flailing Fitzgerald, DeLong witnessed some of his finest performances in the art of official baiting.

"He really played that role well," DeLong said. "He worked them. He was pretty intelligent about it, actually. There were some guys he didn't care for how they worked a game and he let them know it."

Back in Fitzgerald's early days, he could be absolutely intimidating to recalcitrant Zag players. DeLong recalled one player who challenged Fitzgerald ... and almost was physically booted from the team.

"It was going to be a fight," DeLong said. "We grabbed him or it would have been a brawl. He told this kid to put his shoes down and empty his locker and never come back. He was gone."

What DeLong recalls seeing of Fitzgerald in the early days was a dedication—20 hours a day when necessary—to making something of the Gonzaga basketball program.

"When he got here, it was in shambles," DeLong said. "An unbelievable mess. No one can imagine how bad it was. And he righted that ship and created some avenues that led to what we're doing now. It was the framework of why this works so well. It's a shame it ended up the way it did."

Throwing Fitz

Since some of the officials who worked GU basketball games were baseball coaches in their day jobs, GU baseball coach Steve Hertz knew many of them well. They often would meet Hertz for lunch on days they worked Zag games.

Some of them revealed to Hertz their tactics for dealing with Zag coach Dan Fitzgerald, who was known to work over the officials when they came within shouting distance.

"They talked about how they planned to stay on the other side of the court from Fitz," Hertz said. "One of them told me one time that he kind of forgot where he was and he ended up right in Fitz's pocket. Fitz started yelling at him even though he had just made a call that favored the Zags."

The official recalled that he was incredulous, and finally just asked Fitzgerald why in the world he was yelling at him.

"He said that Fitz shook his head," Hertz said. "And just said, 'I don't know, but you were right here and I figured I didn't want to waste the chance.'"

Da Plane, Da Plane

Jamie Dudley (Zag, '93) was listed at five foot nine, a fact coach Dan Fitzgerald didn't overlook.

One game in The Kennel against Loyola Marymount, the Zags were getting thundered at halftime. Geoff Goss recalled Fitzgerald's detonation inside the locker room.

"Fitz was so pissed he chucked the ice chest at the chalkboard and the thing cracked down the middle," Goss said. "But it was hilarious; he looked at the stat sheet and screams: 'We've only got six #$%^&# rebounds and Tattoo here has five of them.'"

Tattoo, in this case, was the diminutive Dudley, whom Fitzgerald decided at that moment resembled the tiny actor who played on Fantasy Island.

"He's so mad, and we couldn't laugh," Goss said. "But it was hilarious the conniption fit he was throwing."

Zag Quip

Behind the 27 points of Jeff Brown and the defensive play of Geoff Goss, who held Stanford All-American Brevin Knight scoreless, the Zags had just registered their first postseason win in school history, an 80-76 NIT road victory over Stanford in 1994. Coach Dan Fitzgerald congratulated them on their effort, addressed a few specifics, urged them to hustle up to get on the bus, and then turned back to them for an important reminder about being good guests.

"Hey, before you go," he said. "Clean up this locker room; these people have been good to us, so let's be sure not to leave a mess."

CHAPTER THIRTEEN

Zags Help

A Game, a Hat, a Memory

Zack Camarda already had figured out some competitive tricks. When Gonzaga basketball players came to visit him at the children's hospital in Spokane, he whipped each in turn at a motocross video game. See, Zack knew a way to kick his opponent off his vehicle at the start of the race. They all laughed when he pulled the stunt.

Ronny Turiaf and Zack hit it off particularly well, Turiaf a six-foot-10 All-America player from the Caribbean with his flowing mop of hair and brilliant future, Zack only age eight, dealing with the daily challenges of a rare form of cancer.

A week after the hospital visit, the Zags invited Zack to be a ball boy for a special game, the night that John Stockton's number was going to be retired late in the 2004 season. After the game, Turiaf ripped the headband off teammate Tony Skinner and gave it to Zack, who, along with his father Bill, was invited into the locker room for a postgame visit.

Turiaf rounded up a ball cap for Zack with all the players' signatures. He disappeared for a few moments, and when he returned, the hat also bore John Stockton's rare autograph.

Gonzaga fans were glad Ronny Turiaf decided to hang around for the 2004-2005 season.

"I left there with tears in my eyes," Bill Camarda said. "From start to finish, that team made sure Zack knew this all was entirely from the heart; it was about nothing but pure motives and kindness. They were unbelievable."

Zack died in the late summer of 2004.

"It chokes me up to say it, but of the things that my son and I did together, that night was the pinnacle of our relationship," Bill Camarda said.

Bill once secretly overheard Zack talking to one of his friends. The friend asked if he was going to die from cancer. Zack defiantly offered: "No way." The friend asked if he hated cancer. Zack admitted that, yes, he did. He truly hated cancer.

"But then he said, 'Yeah, I hate cancer, but I like all the nice things people do for me,'" Bill Camarda said. "I know that the Gonzaga team was a big piece of that. They made a difference for Zack. From a parental standpoint, the night at that game was the best night of our lives together. I can't speak highly enough how it came from those guys' hearts. That will be forever in my memory."

Coaches Versus Cancer

Behind the impetus of Mark and Marcy Few, the Spokane Coaches versus Cancer Gala raised $850,000 through events in its first three years. Some of the funds provide "scholarships" to Camp Good Times, a weeklong camp for kids with cancer. One of the highlights of the week is "Zag Day," said Jerid Keefer, director of the Coaches versus Cancer event.

"In the time I've been rounding up players to go to the oncology ward or getting them to go do readings at elementary schools, I've never had one of them tell me 'no,'" Keefer said. "These guys are college students and they're players and they're busy. But no one has ever turned me down. Not once."

Keeping up Appearances

Although the demands, from genuine to frivolous, start to stack up, Ronny Turiaf stays busy trying to make himself available to good causes.

"Ronny may be as good as we've ever had since I've been here," Mark Few said. "He's unbelievable with people. He knows every secretary in every office and he's always running off somewhere to go watch somebody's daughter in a soccer game or somebody else's son in a school play. We've had some great guys who took interest in doing things for other people, but Ronny has been truly amazing."

Turiaf can't be everywhere, but he takes this unofficial ambassadorship seriously.

"It's important because I know how people feel about the Gonzaga program; they want to be a part of it and I try to be as accessible as I can," he said. "I can't do everything all the time and please everybody, but I do my best and try to do a good job of making people feel good and show them that playing basketball at Gonzaga isn't only about basketball."

Spending time with sick kids is tough, Turiaf said, because it's difficult to see their pain.

"The reward is to see a smile on their face," he said. "I know it's a tough time for them and I feel good if I can make them feel better for a while. When they're having a hard time, it makes me want to try harder to help and let them know I will be there to do whatever I can."

Dan Dickau is another who was in steady demand while at GU.

"At Gonzaga, it's like you're the main deal in the town. We got a lot of attention in Spokane and people were really excited to watch us and meet us. So, we spent a lot of time making appearances and going to hospitals and talking to kids for hours.

"Nobody ever had a problem doing that because it comes down to appreciating the blessings you have and if you can do something to brighten somebody else's day, then a lot of us took it very seriously."

The returns are significant. "It's not something you can measure, of course, but it's a good feeling that somebody actually enjoys your company and cares enough about you to want to spend time with you," Dickau said. "It gives you perspective; You see a kid having a hard time and facing struggles, and you understand that, as a college athlete, you've got it pretty good. You remember that you're one of the real lucky ones."

Heroic Response

Scott Snider snagged a summer job with the Spokane City Parks Department in the early 1990s that included the usual mundane rote of field maintenance and landscaping. With the state softball tournament coming up, his duties on one drizzly morning included preparing the fields for play.

Given the misty conditions, it seemed strange to him that a woman would be on the tennis courts by herself, digging into several duffle bags she had carried. Moments later, Snider saw flames engulf the woman, who ran wildly across the court.

"Adrenaline took over for me, and I ran over to her," Snider said. "I took off my sweatshirt and tried to extinguish the flames. She had run probably 20 feet from where she started and had fallen face first right in front of me. I beat at the flames with my sweatshirt, but her whole body was in flames. I knew she was dead, but I kept trying to kill the fire."

Snider quickly saw that this was no accident as several gas containers and road flares were burning on the court where the woman had placed her bags.

A stunned boss told Snider to take the rest of the day, heck, the rest of the week off. "But I didn't want to do that because I knew I'd just go home and think about it," he said. "I ended up staying and getting all the fields done that day and working a 10-hour shift."

Snider came away conflicted by the episode.

"At first, I was pissed at the lady for doing that in a public place," he said. "There was a young woman walking by with her two little girls when this woman was pouring gas on herself."

Several other city employees who watched Snider's attempt at saving the woman took time off in the aftermath. Snider just kept working. "They kept asking me if I needed counseling," he said. "But the only thing I requested throughout the whole thing was a new sweatshirt."

Snider ended up with a letter of commendation from the Spokane city manager.

And, finally, a replacement sweatshirt.

To Be or Not to Be?

The spreading contagion of Zag fervor has created some demands on ball players. They've done the readings at schools and special appearances and charitable work. But the requests are sometimes far more personal.

"The public wants a piece of these guys, not because they're great basketball players, but because they're really good guys, too," said GU athletic director Mike Roth. "Sometimes, people just call up and want them to show up."

To do what?

"Just to be," Roth said. "They'll call and ask if Ronny Turiaf can come to their daughter's birthday party. Or somebody will write and say that their son is a big fan of fill-in-the-blank player, can he come over to the house?"

Roth keeps an eye on the requests for a specific reason: "These are such good guys, they'd probably do them all and end up having a great time," he said. "The reason the public has glommed onto them so hard is that they see them as regular people as well as basketball players, and that's a huge compliment to them and to the program."

Collecting the Sheepskin

Like a proud parent, athletic director Mike Roth recalled the graduation ceremonies of the class of 2004.

"We had five [basketball players] graduate," Roth said. "But it wasn't just them getting the degree that was impressive ... all five were there to walk across the stage to get the diploma along with their classmates. I think that shows that they don't see themselves as different or above the regular students. And I think it says something about the experience they had here off the court."

Which, apparently, included attending classes.

CHAPTER FOURTEEN

"Q"

Bahama Surprise

The scouts at the prep tournament in Las Vegas focused on touted Seattle guard Jason Terry. His quickness and court savvy would land him a ride to Arizona and a ticket to the NBA. But some keen-eyed talent assessors spotted one player who was even quicker, at least as fiercely competitive ... and uncommitted.

The hidden gem was small, just five foot eight, and hailed from the Bahamas, an out-of-the-way source for basketball talent.

Leon Rice, then coach at Yakima Valley College, leaned over to Mark Few, his friend and future boss at GU.

"God, Mark, you've got to recruit this kid," Rice said after seeing Quentin Hall hound Terry step for step. "Nobody knew anybody on that Bahamas team, but this kid was really something."

Few followed up, and went through the sacrifice of traveling to the Caribbean island to personally recruit Hall.

"It was like that movie with Kevin Bacon [*The Air Up There*] where he goes to Africa to look at a guy," Few said. "We set up this trip and the place is unbelievable. There's no air conditioning and there's all these hot little outbuildings. It's 95 degrees and 90 percent humidity and I'm in this blazer and shirt and tie ... a big mistake."

Dripping sweat, Few trundled into a blazing building to try to figure out Hall's academic standing, and then retreated courtside to watch practice. Outdoors. Under a merciless sun.

On a court that put out heat waves like a griddle.

"These guys are going at it like you can't believe on outdoor blacktop," Few said. "I'm profusely sweating, and these guys are diving for loose balls on hot blacktop."

Hall's first impression of Few was of this sweaty guy who was definitely out of place wearing his coach's "uniform" there in the sweltering islands.

"It was very funny," Hall said. "He came to one of my practices with that long-sleeved shirt and tie. The sun was blazing hot and my teammates and I looked at him and wondered, 'Is he SERIOUS?'"

One could imagine at that point that Few's recruiting efforts might have reached snowball-in-hell odds. But he certainly knew he liked what he saw in Hall.

One problem: Hall couldn't get into Gonzaga academically, so he was set up to work toward his Associate Arts degree at nearby North Idaho College in Coeur d'Alene. The understanding was that he'd join the Zags after two years.

Another surprise arose to alter the script. The GU staff had gathered in the field house atrium for coach Bill Grier's wedding reception in late August of 1996. While guests mingled and celebrated the nuptials, a tearful Quentin Hall arrived to inform the staff that NIC had sent him home. Rice, among the revelers, recognized Hall from the Las Vegas tournament, and quickly jumped in. Do NOT get on that plane, he urged Hall. He'd gladly find a spot for him at Yakima Valley.

YVC didn't offer aid to athletes, though, and Hall worked as a dorm janitor to pay his bills. "It was really a sacrifice for him to stay a year at Yakima, but he busted his butt so hard it was amazing. You could really see his dedication to making it work."

But Hall almost blew an audition when YVC came to Spokane Community College for a game that the entire Gonzaga staff scouted. Rice's team separated early, held its lead and Hall was virtually invisible.

"To their credit, none of them said, 'Oh, this kid isn't good enough' or anything like that," Rice said. "So Dan [Monson] took it upon himself to come see our next game, and Quentin put on a show, with 35 points and 15 assists. That pretty much convinced Dan."

Big Gamesmanship

Quentin Hall showed up with the mentality of a fearless little terrier, snapping and yapping and nipping at the flanks of any opponent within range, irrespective of size or reputation. No, actually, the bigger the renown, the more appealing the target for Hall.

He broke down opponents with his quickness, with his ferocity, and with his gamesmanship if necessary, worming his way into their minds, nibbling off chunks of their confidence.

"Quentin has a way with him," coach Leon Rice said. "He's just an absolute tiger; he doesn't care who he's playing against or whether it's in the NCAA Tournament or wherever."

The protocol, during pregame introductions at NCAA games, calls for a player from one team to take the floor and shake hands with his opposing counterpart. It's meant to be a nice gesture of sportsmanship before the serious hostilities begin. Not for Hall, however.

"He would go out there and the guy would hold his hand out, and Quentin would just slap that thing as hard as he could," Bill Grier said. "You could see these guys look at him like, 'What in the world are you doing?'"

Against Connecticut in the 1999 Regional Final, Hall was matched against All-America Husky point guard Khalid El-Amin. For Hall, this was a delicious setup; a big-time guy who never heard of Quentin Hall, and who likely had no hint in the world that he was about to be struck by a rolling ball of butcher knives.

Hall's assault started even before tip off. "He went out there and walked right through UConn's stretching circle," Grier said.

Hall executed one crossover move that almost caused El-Amin to break an ankle as he fell to the court in a futile attempt to recover from the misdirection.

In the end, UConn won, although it was a one-point game until the final 35 seconds. Hall finished with 18 points and eight rebounds, to easily outplay El-Amin, who was harassed into an 0-for-12 shooting night.

Q Has the A

If the Zags were to win their first-round NCAA Tournament game in 1999 against Minnesota at Seattle's KeyArena, they needed to find a way to negate the Gophers' six-foot-seven All-America forward Quincy Lewis. Turns out, he was as easy to solve as the Monday crossword.

The GU staff threw something at Lewis that he could have never expected ... a five foot eight showstopper named Quentin Hall. They designed a Box-and-1 configuration that left four Zags in a zone, and Hall to attach himself to Lewis no matter where he went.

The vision was almost comical, as the mismatched Hall crawled up inside Lewis's jersey like a parasite and harassed him without clemency.

"It was just me being me and having fun talking trash like I normally did," Hall said. "He really didn't say much, but I was letting him know that he was not [worthy] of all the hype that he got. Just fun talk."

The unusual pairing reminded coach Mark Few of the old Foghorn Leghorn cartoon where the chunky pullet is mercilessly beset by a minuscule chicken hawk unwilling to recognize the improbability of his instinctive mandate to attack the bigger foe.

"Quentin was the chicken hawk that game," Few said.

Casey Calvary listened to Hall's comical verbal assault of Lewis, and heard different segments and installments every time Lewis and Hall entered his hearing radius.

"He chatted him up the whole time," Calvary said. "He kept saying things like, 'They say you're NBA, but you're no NBA, you're garbage.'"

Lewis, the Big Ten Conference's leading scorer, finished with eight points on a miserable three-for-19 shooting performance.

Coach Dan Monson recalled that the Zags originally had prepared a triangle-and-two defense (a suggestion of his father, Don, "a master at junk defenses," he said), but suspensions of top Gopher players left only Lewis as a primary threat, so they settled on the box-and-1. The tenacious Hall, of course, was the "1."

"I remember one time when they came over for a time out, Q told me, 'Stay in de box, Coach, he is scared-a me,'" Monson said.

"He got so far inside Quincy Lewis's head it was unbelievable," Few said. "It was non-stop chatter."

Apparently, you would expect nothing less from a chicken hawk.

Forever Q

Quentin Hall continues to battle current Zags in open-gym games, and while the quickness of the feet has lapsed, the competitive commentary remains as corrosive as ever.

"Now that he's lost a couple steps, his game is now total mental warfare," Mark Few said. "He not only tries to manipulate the opponent with his talk, he really pumps up his teammates. 'They can't stop you, big man; they're helpless against you.'"

The chatter, of course, isn't limited to the court, as Hall continues to assault Bill Grier for his dietary choices, although Grier remains trim.

"He's always saying something like, 'Oh, Billy Bob, you're looking a little thick, should you be having that extra serving?'" Few said with a laugh. "And for a while, he was always telling me that I was going to be done as soon as Casey [Calvary] left. He was a classic; it was great having him around."

You Are or You Aren't

Mark Few remembers a little quiz game that Quentin Hall created. It was a simple binary evaluation of a basketball player's skills.

"Quentin had this game with Richie Frahm," Few said. "Richie would throw out a name and Quentin would decide whether the player was a 'baller' or a 'buster.' A 'baller' could play; a 'buster' couldn't."

Quentin Hall? Baller. And if you were a buster, he'd be sure to let you hear about it.

Zag Myth: Q Busts Up UConn's Huddle

Casey Calvary laughs as he tells this story. His primary memory of the West Regional championship game against Connecticut in March of 1999 was not of the team's nearness to the Final Four, not of his individual efforts ... but of Quentin Hall's brash bravado.

"Here we are, playing the No. 1 team in the nation and we're supposed to be in awe of them, but not Quentin," Calvary said. "I'll never forget right before the game when each team gets in a huddle and everybody puts their hands in and then breaks on a call. They all had their hands in and Q squeezed in there and says: 'We're about to bust y'all's asses ... ass-bustin' on 3.'"

So, Quentin Hall, is that accurate?

"Yeah, it's true," Hall admitted. "I did go in the huddle and say 'Busters,' just a phrase that I used when I felt we could beat a team ... which was probably every game."

Q: Being a Zag

The notion of giving up life on a Caribbean island to go to school in the meteorologically intemperate Spokane, Washington was radical enough. But when the coach showed up on his recruiting trip to the islands practically dressed in a parka, Hall, naturally, was skeptical.

"But little did I know he was bringing me to a wonderful family like the Gonzaga family," Hall said. "The special thing about being a Zag is that everybody is loyal and cares about what happens on and off the court. For that team that went to the Elite Eight, I can say that we did well because we all got along with each other on and off the court."

As of the fall of 2004, Hall lived in Holland, where he'd continued playing for five seasons.

"It's been ups and downs, but an experience that has made me a better person," he said. "Of course, I'll always be a Bulldog, and trust me, those who didn't know it, I make sure they do."

Dat Coach Quit on Dem

Gonzaga was putting together the final points on a win over Clemson in the Top of the World Classic title game in November of 1997, and Clemson coach Rick Barnes hadn't been overjoyed with the officiating. The Zags took possession in the final minute with a 13-point lead, and Quentin Hall heard Barnes at the other end of the floor telling his team not to foul, symbolic of waving the white flag of surrender.

"Quentin dribbled the ball over to me to tell me something," coach Dan Monson said, going into his impersonation of Hall's lilting Bahamian accent. "He said, 'Coach, dat coach has quit on dem. Don't you eva do dat to us. We neva outta da game.'

"More than any kid I ever coached, that's the kind of attitude he brought to every game, to every practice," Monson said. "His mindset about winning was unparalleled."

Monson tells a story that indicates Hall's innate love of pressure situations.

"He was sitting in my office after he finally got eligible after going to summer school," Monson said. "I knew he hadn't played much basketball because he had been in class. I asked when he'd last played. He said, 'Oh, it's been a long time, but I tell you dis Coach, if you need me to go down dere and make a basket for you right now, I do it. Dat ball is goin' in de hole right now.'"

Monson didn't challenge Hall on the matter. He'd have plenty of time to prove it in games.

CHAPTER FIFTEEN

Riddle of the Spinks

The Family Spink

Scott Spink got it started. Whippet thin but able to bound over the rim, he came out of Bellingham to join a group of freshmen redshirts who regularly waxed the varsity during the lamentable 8-20 season of 1990. That group, Spink included, would put the Zags in their first postseason tournament, visiting the NIT in 1994.

Brother Tomson Spink arrived when Scott was a junior, and when he didn't manage to stick with the team as a walk-on, he became the most vocal, most outrageous member of The Kennel Club.

Sister Theresa was a Zag volleyball player at GU.

And finally, with a personality that paled the quirky, expressive characters who preceded him through the Gonzaga ranks, came forward/comedian Mark Spink. If Casey Calvary was the backbone of some of GU's most accomplished NCAA Tournament teams, Mark Spink was the funny bone.

All were gifted students and postgraduate successes. What must the home life been like for this group? "It was awesome," Scott Spink said. "My parents had five kids before they were 31, so you do the math ... they grew up WITH us."

Father Tom was a chemical engineer, and mother MaryEllen had such a powerful faith that she fully expected Scott to join the priesthood.

"It all stemmed from my parents," Mark Spink said of their individualistic perspective. "My dad played a little basketball and track at Seattle U. A lot of it comes from my mom. And a lot of it has to do with us beating the shit out of each other when we were kids. We were a big family and we were competitive and I was introduced to athletics through big brothers who were mentors to me."

Family discussions might focus on business or politics or literature ... and they were unwaveringly thought provoking. "We'd have the most amazing conversations because they were all blessed with humor and are intelligent and well-spoken," Mark Spink said.

Scott got two degrees from Gonzaga, one in engineering and one in business, and as of the fall of 2004, was involved in product development for a company trying to design "commercial fuel cells for back-up power applications."

Mark, finding a profession that seems a bit dry for his ebullient personality, was an accountant in Portland.

And Tomson? His evolution was the most startling and unpredictable of all. As of October 2004, as a well-respected engineer, he was the project manager for the construction of the Zags' new $25-million on-campus arena.

Electric Gatorade

Living in a dorm room with the hyperkinetic Geoff Goss was "like being trapped in one of those little running cages with a squirrel," said Scott Spink. But Spink saw Goss slow down at least once.

"You can't have alcohol in the dorms, but of course we did," Spink said. "And we got caught a couple times, too. I came home from a party one night with about half a fifth of vodka and I knew I had to get rid of the bottle so we wouldn't get busted again."

Spink, using the problem-solving logic that allowed him to get an engineering degree from Gonzaga, poured the vodka into the

Gatorade he had in his dorm refrigerator, chucked the bottle out the window, and stumbled off to bed to try to salvage a little shut-eye before a scrimmage in the morning.

Meanwhile, Goss returned home from a bibulous night of his own.

"He's smashed, but he knows he's got to get some aspirin and some fluids in him before he goes to bed or else he'll be wrecked for practice," Spink said. "We get up to go, and he is an absolute mess, feeling terrible. I opened the frig ... he drank all my Gatorade ... with all that vodka in it."

Lucky he didn't get alcohol poisoning, isn't it?

"Yeah," Spink said. "I guess we didn't think about that sort of thing much at the time."

Battling Bulldogs

Coaches preach it ceaselessly: You play how you practice. A lax attitude in practices will result in sloppy execution in games. But a combativeness every day in drills will result in a team ready for anything. Or so they love to say.

Gonzaga players have cleaved to the theory over the years, and often wore the black eyes to prove it.

"In five years, I probably saw 10 fistfights in practice," Scott Spink said. "Matt Stanford and I got in a fight one time, and he's a really good friend of mine. I can't remember exactly why; he called a foul or something that wasn't a foul and they won because of it and I wouldn't take it."

In retrospect, Spink sees this willingness to throw down and go at it as one of the most important qualities the team had.

"That's why we were a good team," he said. "Nothing else in our lives mattered but winning. Nobody cared about who got the publicity, nobody cared about who scored, nobody cared about school. Don't take that wrong, Goss has a law degree and I have two degrees from Gonzaga; Brown was the national scholar athlete. But that's not why we went there. We did not go there for the school; we went there to win basketball games."

What was the reaction of the coaching staff to this attitude?

"I think Fitz, in a way, encouraged it to a point," Spink said. "That's kind of how he lived his life. If you're in your mid-50s and you have a group of people who have the same fire and passion and beliefs you do, you can live vicariously through them. Sometimes he'd throw his head back and laugh."

The Few, the Proud, the Zags

Asked to evaluate the evolution of the Gonzaga program, Scott Spink cited the fact that "Mark Few may be the best judge of talent in the country."

"Who's the last player they missed on?" Spink asked rhetorically. "If they miss on somebody, the guy doesn't stay around. That didn't used to happen; Fitz always just kept guys, and that's made a big difference."

Aside from better talent and the addition of some roster churn, Few has changed the mindset.

"His attitude is: We can beat anybody ... anybody," Spink said. "That's why they're as good as they are. They don't accept playing well and losing. That didn't come from Fitz. With Fitz, it was sometimes okay to play well and lose. These guys don't tolerate playing well and losing."

The landing of Casey Calvary, too, was a critical development.

"He was such an animal in there," Spink said. "For him, it really wasn't okay to lose; he wouldn't stand for it."

Scott Spink: Being a Zag

Having been a part of Gonzaga basketball—participant or observer—for 15 seasons, Scott Spink sees a couple common denominators in those who preceded and those who followed.

"They tend to be genuinely good people," Spink said. "You'd have a hard time finding a bad apple in the group."

At Gonzaga players share same experiences ... and that includes going to the classroom.

"You're not sequestered from the students, you live with them," Spink said. "I know the guys who have come through here have done the same things and been through the same things that I have. They know what it takes to get through, to play, to go to school, to make it all work. We all have a lot in common. So I care about how Casey Calvary is doing; if he does well it speaks well for the tradition and it makes the rest of us look good when anybody does good, too."

He Ain't Brittle, He's My Brother

In his first practice of his junior season, Scott Spink suffered a curious injury (collision, brother).

Before having a real chance to welcome younger brother Tomson to the team, Scott was flattened by the aggressive sibling.

"He broke my leg," Scott Spink said. "I ended up missing most of the preseason because of it."

Tomson cops to the charges.

"Scott was a little quicker and a little better jumper, and I was known for clubbing people," Tomson said. "I clubbed him. I didn't mean to hurt him; he jumped and I ran him over ... his knee happened to be in the way. As a family, we never fight, we're very nice and we care about each other."

Clubbing aside, evidently.

"He wasn't mad," Tomson said. "I apologized and he accepted it and we were okay."

An Engineering Marvel

Tomson Spink racked up imposing statistics in high school, but at Gonzaga, the basketball career reached a cul-de-sac and he detoured in the direction of The Kennel Club, injecting it with spirit and rowdiness.

But he claims he was never officially ejected from a game.

"I love basketball and I love Gonzaga," Tomson Spink said. "Basketball is a passion for me."

Some of the chants, language and gestures emanating from The Kennel Club under Spink's provocation, though, were not well-received by all university administrators.

"Yeah, it got a little over the top sometimes," Spink said. "We drank a lot of beers, which may have led to some of the problems. I never actually got kicked out. I was never actually escorted or removed from any games. I was probably pretty close some times."

At times, Scott Spink watched the cavalcade of tomfoolery from the floor or the bench.

"He was pretty crazy, yeah," Scott Spink said. "All I would say is that everybody's entitled to their discovery. He is different than me. But all of us are totally different."

Mark Spink saw Tomson's notorious exploits as the result of a common college syndrome. "I think there were a lot of beers involved," he said. "His personality is such that he likes to question and he likes to challenge. He always plays the devil's advocate and gets in people's faces. You throw some booze into that mix and it makes for an interesting combination."

But not one that is permanent.

"He's been dealt a couple really difficult situations," Mark said. "But his head is set squarely on his shoulders and it's great that he is the project manager on the new arena. It's great that Scott and I could play in The Kennel and Tomson can work on building the new one."

Tomson recognizes the irony in his situation, but took so much pride in the project and felt so much responsibility, he said, that it was extremely stressful.

"My name is associated with probably the biggest project Gonzaga has had in a long time," Tomson said. "It's hard to accept anything but doing the best on something this important. The company teases me a lot because I freak out about the quality of it, but I want it to be nice."

Athletic director Mike Roth, director of facilities at the time of Tomson's most obstreperous exploits, had numerous confrontations trying to get him to take the edge off his fierce fanhood. "If anybody had told us at the time that Tomson Spink one day would be in charge of building the new arena, we would have run away at full speed," Roth said. "But we couldn't be more delighted with the job he's done. He's been wonderful."

Last of the Spinks

Mark Spink saw the experience his brother Scott had playing at Gonzaga, having fun, winning games, building close friendships. He naturally sought the same.

"That group that my brother was with, Jamie Dudley, Geoff Goss, Jeff Brown ... I think they turned the first corner for Gonzaga basketball. To see his interactions with those people and the friendships he made just made me want to be a part of that environment."

He remembered the unimposing vita emanating from his first physical as a GU freshman: He was six foot seven, 169 pounds. "The rigors of Division I basketball don't tend to lend themselves to guys who are that size," Spink said.

Although built like a 1-iron, Mark Spink left a legacy that transcended his scoring or rebounding totals. Ask players of Spink's vintage to name a character or a powerful personality or the best teammate, and they unanimously say "Mark Spink." And then they start laughing.

The coaches, though, follow the laughter, quickly, with laudatory comments regarding his intense play.

"Mark Spink was the heart and soul of what we were all about," coach Mark Few said. "Spink would go in there and scrap out a rebound against a Mark Madsen, or tip-dunk on somebody he had no business beating. That sort of thing demoralized other teams. You could write an entire book on the things he did here. He loved to say and do outlandish things, but on the court he came to play. He was fearless and never cared if he went out there and killed his body.

*Mark Spink (Zag, '01) was always focused on the court,
but was known for his antics away from it.*

When the game was over, though, he was just so intelligent and so witty that it was a joy to be around him."

In Mark Spink, assistant coach Tommy Lloyd saw a fierce competitor who didn't take himself too seriously. A guy who loved winning, but who wasn't as single-mindedly devoted to basketball as some others.

"He was incredibly intelligent, with such a tremendous perspective on things," Lloyd said. "He took a lot of pride in being a well-rounded person, an academic, being social and having friends outside of basketball. He was not one of those guys who were going to be down at the gym all night working on his game. But he knew his job on the court and he did it. He constantly would take people out of their games, contorting his body or throwing himself at bigger guys just to frustrate them."

It was said that Mark Spink would do anything to help the Zags win. Anything but be ordinary, or predictable, or quiet.

Best Teammate: Mark Spink

Hands down, no contest, Mark Spink left a greater legacy at GU than many players who scored three times the number of points.

"This guy was the best teammate ever," Dan Dickau said. "He was a comedian, just unbelievably funny. Most college basketball players on scholarship are expected to spend their summers working out; he never did. And nobody minded because when he showed up for the first day of conditioning, he'd work harder than anybody else and you knew when he stepped on the floor, he was going to give you everything he had."

Ryan Floyd roomed with Spink on the road. Which is to say he had a front-row seat at the circus.

"Mark is a very free individual; very independent and a wild ball of energy that you never know which direction he's going to go," Floyd said. "He was such an incredible guy. He's the nicest guy in the world, but he just bounces off the wall with energy."

Spink was never the most talented player, nor the most imposing. "But for his size, he made way more of himself than just about
anybody," Floyd said. "He was fearless and he played with pure
heart. He was so smart, he knew what his weaknesses were, but he
learned how to hide them. Whenever he came on the floor, you
could feel the energy level of every one of us go up. That's a rare
thing."

The job Spink did against the powerful Mark Madsen in the
NCAA Tournament win over Stanford in 1999 was an instance
where he inspired his teammates.

"He was just a great leader, always a guy who was getting us
pumped up," Casey Calvary said. "If something was going wrong,
he'd be a vocal leader, he was so aggressive on the boards. For somebody who didn't lift a ton of weights or shoot a lot of jump shots,
when things were on the line, he was in there doing it. He was Mr.
Floor Burn, always diving, getting loose balls, defending people,
making stops. Everybody who played with him sure appreciated the
effort he put out."

The Name Game

Comedy can be tough. Some of the recipients of Mark Spink's
wicked nicknames were less than flattered by the attention.

Cory Violette didn't particularly care for the tag "Manatee," and
Blake Stepp was not keen on being labeled "Helmet."

"I like coming up with nicknames and I thought "Manatee" was
a great one because when Cory came in, he was a huge dude, an
18-year-old who was 250 pounds," Spink said. "He was a strong guy
who hadn't spent a lot of time in the weight room and was a little
soft around the edges, you might say. Plus, his nature was to be a
really mellow guy, so it fit."

So, Violette enjoyed being compared to a one-ton slothful sea
mammal?

"He hated it," Spink said. "He was livid. He wouldn't say
anything directly to us because Casey [Calvary] was the strong arm
of the law and he was always there to back me up."

Helmet?

Mark Spink contended that the toughest Zag he played with was Mike Nilson (background). Stephen Dunn/Getty Images

"When he came in, Blake had this terrible Eddie Munster-type hair cut," Spink said. "The name bothered him for a while until he got used to my personality. And then, before every game, I used to make a sign to him like buckling up the chin strap on a helmet, like, it's time to go get 'em."

The kidding of Violette, Spink said, was more than just cruel comedy; it was meant as incentive.

"It was a practical joke, sure, but if there were times in practice when he wasn't giving it his all and maybe getting beat by guys who weren't as good as he was, then we'd call him 'Manatee' and it meant get your ass in gear. He took it to heart."

Unsung Zag: Carl Crider

Coming from tiny Tekoa-Oakesdale, and transferring in from Eastern Washington, Carl Crider was of limited portfolio but unlimited grit.

"This was a guy who never got much playing time and played behind a bunch of good guards," Mark Spink said. "But he was just a tough guy who never let the fact that other players were more heavily recruited affect how he approached the game. He was one of those second-tier guys like me and Mike Nilson and Ryan Floyd who all looked at Carl and said, 'Hey, if he's not giving up, the rest of us can't either.'"

Spink's Toughest Zag: Mike Nilson

Mark Spink spent a lot of time in the paint being pinballed around by the powerful Casey Calvary, but for the toughest teammate he could name, it was Mike Nilson, whom he claims to be the strongest man, pound for pound, he'd ever seen.

"When he popped his Achilles' tendon, there was hardly a tear out of the guy," Spink said. "All he said was, 'My season is done, you guys have to step it up.' That just showed the mental toughness this guy had."

Nilson brought a fearlessness to the floor, too, that won over and inspired his teammates.

"Mike wouldn't hesitate to challenge anybody, even Casey, because he was a guy who was willing to get his nose dirty and would call guys out if they weren't playing as hard as they could play."

Night at the Improv

So, for all the talk about how comical Mark Spink was, what's the best Spink story former roommate Ryan Floyd can tell?

"I don't think there's really ANY that I can tell."

Okay, a few sanitized versions: There was the night when postgame celebrations concluded with Spink swimming in the koi pond of a swanky San Diego hotel.

And there was the time he apparently felt that there was still a portion of the Spokane County populace who had not yet seen him naked, so he entered the famous Bare Buns Fun Run. The neon white Spink stood nude at the starting line for half an hour before being informed that the race wasn't until the following day.

And one that is colorful but more tasteful: Before the Zags played in the West Regional in Arizona in 2000, Spink made a shortsighted decision about his appearance.

"Because I'm one of the pastier men around, especially during a Spokane winter, I tried putting on some of that fake tanning stuff to take the edge off the whiteness," Spink said. "I had never done it before and I put the whole bottle on my body. It was such a stupid thing to do. I showed up for the game and I was ORANGE."

Mark Spink: Being a Zag

It starts from the minute a recruit arrives at Gonzaga. If he fits in, he's adopted.

"It's not only how good a player a guy is, but it's his attitude toward school; is he going to be a guy you want to be around," Mark

Spink said. "It was our job to interact with the kid and see if he would fit in. We'd go out and b.s. with other students and see how they interacted; see how they hold themselves; see how they treated women."

So, often, the critical elements of becoming a Zag had little to do with basketball skills.

"It's way more than basketball," Spink said. "I hope that's coming across. I can't reiterate that enough. There's so much more to the experience than that. It has to do with being around a lot of guys you will cherish as friends for a long time."

Chapter Sixteen

"Doctor" DeLong

Keeping Them Flying

Trainers know players far better than the coaches do. A player will try to hide physical weaknesses from a coach, but he will let a trainer in on it to seek swift solutions. So, the job of the trainer goes beyond taping ankles and monitoring the whirlpool as he evolves into counselor, father confessor and confidant.

"There's an element of trust there, no question," longtime GU trainer Steve DeLong said. "The thing is, we all want the same thing. The athletes want to be healthy and back on the court as soon as possible. But none of us wants them to be crippled when they're 30, either. And players often don't have an understanding of their future."

DeLong fiercely guards their confidences and conditions, but when pressed to pinpoint the Zag with the highest pain threshold, he mentions Blake Stepp.

"Blake is a tough kid who went through a lot in his career," DeLong said. "Starting back in high school, there were some things he played through that most people could never have done. He just always found a way to get it done."

At times, Stepp could hardly practice, and DeLong would intercede on his behalf with the coaches.

"I used to ask, 'Well, do you want him ready for the practices, or do you want him ready for the games?'" DeLong said.

Easy choice, there.

Gospel from the Book of Steve

Steve DeLong sat on the Gonzaga bench longer than anybody, 25 consecutive years, in fact. Quiet and effective, DeLong and his efforts probably went unnoticed by most Zag basketball fans. But not the staff and players.

"How many programs in the country would have a trainer who has the impact Steve DeLong has?" coach Mark Few asked. "He gets between guys' ears; he toughens them up and he calms the staff down. He's a real important buffer. He might say, 'You're going a little too hard now, maybe you should ease up a little about now.'"

Does the staff listen?

"We treat his word like it's the gospel," Few said.

Zag Myth: Get Me Well ... Or You Die

The story is passed down as an example of Zag toughness, however unreasonable or overstated. Supposedly, Ken Anderson, who would go on to be a respected member of the Gonzaga business school faculty and the school's NCAA faculty representative, threatened trainer Steve DeLong with murder if he failed to "heal" him before a big game.

True enough.

Warming up before a game at San Francisco, Anderson slipped on the court and suffered a groin strain. He'd been fending off some leg troubles at the time, but this was more significant.

"We got into the locker room, and he tells me that if he doesn't play, he's going to kill me," DeLong said. "Really, it wasn't just a kidding sort of tone, either. It was like, 'Listen, I'm playing or I'm coming after you.'"

Actually, Anderson recalled saying, "If you don't make me right in the next five minutes, I'm going to #$%&# kill you," he said. "We were fighting to get to the NCAAs and I was not going to miss that game. Steve took it very seriously."

Benefiting from the taping job of DeLong's life, Anderson played the entire game.

Travels with Steve

Especially in the old days, you had to be versatile at Gonzaga. So, Steve DeLong was not only trainer—with all the diverse duties that title implied—but he also handled some of the travel plans for the team.

Which, when GU was a shoestring operation, carried some challenges.

"One time we showed up in Los Angeles and the hotel marquee read: 'Welcome, Gonzaga,'" DeLong said. "But when we went to check in, they didn't have our rooms. We said, 'We're Gonzaga.' And they said, 'Who?'"

Pointing to the marquee didn't help. It took hours to iron it out.

Another time, when stranded by a snowstorm in Green Bay, rooms were unavailable, so the team and staff slept in a hotel bar, in booths, under tables ... wherever.

When they showed up for rental cars at another city, the clerk at the counter had mistaken the Gonzaga University party for an individual driver named "Mr. Gonzales." When coach Dan Fitzgerald tried to sign for the vehicles, he was denied, since he wasn't "Mr. Gonzales."

"It was always a challenge early," DeLong said, adding that GU's name recognition these days makes travel go much more smoothly. "Now we have hotel security people assigned to help us deal with pressure from fans," he said.

DeLong has no trouble citing the worst experience, back in 1979 when the Zags were still in the Big Sky Conference. They had visited Northern Arizona in Flagstaff, and had bused back to Phoenix to spend the night before hopping their plane the next morning.

"We got to this hotel, a giant place, and it was owned by a bunch of what looked like Mafia guys," DeLong said. "You wouldn't believe this place; on some of the rooms, the doors were broken in. There had been a fire and some of the beams were caved in. Some rooms had no TV, no phone, and some didn't even have bathrooms."

The Mafia didn't scare coach Dan Fitzgerald.

DeLong recalled how Fitzgerald responded to the insult. "We took off in the morning," DeLong said.

Without paying.

DeLong Way Home

The champion of getting thrown out of the training room for his hijinx? Geoff Goss.

"He was a troublemaker," Steve DeLong said. "That group, with Goss and Jeff Brown and Matt Stanford, that era, was probably the most fun group. They were really a unit; they hung together tight and they had a good time together."

It is a reflection of DeLong's dedication to his job, his school, and to that group of guys, that he performed a service beyond the customary role of trainer. He would shepherd his flock home regardless how far it had strayed.

"On the road, the rules were that Saturday night after the game was their time," DeLong said. "All they had to do was make it to the plane Sunday morning. With that group, I used to meet them at a certain place at a certain time to bring them back to the hotel. We didn't want them ending up in a bad spot."

Their condition may have been shaky at times, but they always made it home, DeLong said. They did so, largely, because they respected DeLong so much and didn't want him to get in a bind while serving as unofficial "Den Mother."

Goss won't deny that he won the distinction of being kicked out of the training room by DeLong the most times for unrestrained puckishness, most notably jumping naked from behind a wall into a defensive stance just as the unsuspecting DeLong entered the room. Of course, to Goss, that was an act of respect.

"Steve is probably the most loyal, solid and best person you could ever be around," said Goss, whose naked ambush skills are rarely called for these days as an attorney in Boise. "I think Steve liked how competitive we were. He was a really competitive guy himself and I think he admired that in us. So, he said, hey, if you guys win some games, I'll make sure you stay out of trouble."

Ouch, That Hurts

As the man responsible for apportionment and distribution of new gym shoes, trainer Steve DeLong wielded considerable power in the eyes of players.

"Geoff Goss used to be petrified of Steve," Jeff Brown said. "Steve would always make you show why you needed new shoes; we didn't just get them handed out for no reason. Goss went in there one time, with his real fast, kind of nervous manner of speech and goes, 'Hey, Steve, I ... I ... I need a new pair of shoes.'

"Steve gave him this funny look and asked: 'Do you even play here?'"

DeLong projected that tough façade to newcomers.

"Like blue steel," Mark Spink said. "But then that softens as you get to know him."

"He had the kindest, gentlest heart of anyone," Brown said. "He's the trainer and his job is to make sure guys are healthy and recover from injuries."

But as another of his vital, unseen duties was exuding the quiet expectation of accountability.

"He would never presume to get into Xs and Os or tactics, but he would jump your ass pretty hard if he thought you weren't competing hard," Brown said. "He didn't know all that much about basketball strategy, but he did know what competing was all about, and he took that very seriously."

CHAPTER SEVENTEEN

Songs of the Unsung Zags

Managing Fine, Thanks

Drew Dannels broke the traditional mold of the manager as a guy who hands out towels, washes the jocks and caters to the athletes as if he were a personal manservant at their disposal. They called him "Johnny Utah."

Aaron Hill followed and expanded on Dannels's achievements, although nobody would know him by his given name since his predominantly used nickname around Spokane is "Hobus."

Lucas Rae continued to refine and elevate the product as he went from Gonzaga basketball manager to assistant basketball coach at Emporia State.

Postgraduate success for Rae should not surprise: Dannels is an executive for a high-tech firm in the Seattle area; Hill is Gonzaga's director of marketing and promotions.

Interviews of Gonzaga players from the late 1980s through early 2000s generally ended up with players commenting on the value and importance of their managers in keeping the process running smoothly. The players praised their efficiency and emphasized their roles as part of the team.

Scott Snider, former player and coach, roomed with Dannels for a while and saw the extent of his dedication.

"I thought I put in a lot of time into Gonzaga basketball," Snider said. "But after seeing Drew's dedication and hard work, I have nothing but great respect for managers."

"This is a people place," coach Mark Few said. "I always say that and some can't understand what I mean. But from the athletic department to across campus, to the business school, to the grounds people who work here. There are just a lot of great people at this place."

And some of them started out as managers for the basketball team.

Johnny Utah

Guard Kevin Williams eyeballed the little guy who showed up to be the manager of the basketball team. He was five foot two, and had the temerity to venture into the habitat of creatures nearly two feet taller, most of whom had an appetite for wicked wisecracks and belittling put-downs.

Williams saw on the roster that the new meat was named John Andrew Dannels, and he was from Utah. So he affixed the name "Johnny Utah."

The new manager brought to his job a sense of duty, a sense of humor, and the idea that he was one of the Zags ... maybe a little shorter ... but a Zag nonetheless.

"I did a lot of grunt work, but I never felt like a grunt," Dannels said. "I traveled, I was part of the team and those guys were first class all the way. I give Fitz a lot of the credit for creating a culture in which the manager was treated with so much respect."

Opposing teams and their fans were not so generous, and Dannels was an appealing target.

"We were in Wichita, Kansas, one time at a holiday tournament," Dannels said. "And right when one of their players was going to shoot a free throw and it was real quiet, one of their fans yelled: 'Hey, I've taken shits bigger than your manager.'

"I've got enough confidence in myself and a good enough sense of humor to see that it was funny; our whole bench was cracking up."

Fitzgerald's wit alone was capable of carving up players as if they'd been autopsied, but he and the team understood how important Dannels had become to their daily functioning.

"We ragged on each other all the time, but I know I received three times more compliments than anything else," Dannels said. "The coaches and the guys were entirely respectful and appreciative."

Dannels remembers a day when he truly felt like one of the team: Sore as hell, that is.

"I can't remember what happened in the game that preceded it, but one practice Fitz made the entire team stand up, one by one, and take charges from the rest of the team," Dannels said. "So, he threw me in there, too; I had to stand in there and take charges from the whole team. He did a great job of making me feel like I was a part of everything."

Coach Mark Few marveled at the way Dannels dealt with the players and the fans and the jokes and the jabs.

"He was just an unbelievable individual," Few said. "So giving, so nice. He was so at peace with who he was and what he did; he was just a great, great person."

Wanna Race?

Drew Dannels may have been considerably shorter and less noticeably athletic than the Zag players who were his compatriots in college, but it's fair to suggest he's fitter than any of them in these postgraduate days.

Dannels, who earned a finance and marketing degree from GU (with a 3.9 GPA in his major field), is the business manager for a high-tech company in Redmond, Washington. And he has completed eight marathons and also an Ironman triathlon in North Carolina.

The Ironman test includes a 2.4-mile swim, 112 miles on a bike and a 26.2-mile run.

"Those guys were talented basketball players then," Dannels said. "But I think I could take them in a triathlon."

Why Hobus?

To ask people around the Gonzaga athletic department about Aaron Hill is to draw blank looks and quizzical stares. Aaron Hill is known as "Hobus."

The initial Hobus at Gonzaga was forward Hugh Hobus, who did a lot of baseline dirty work for the Zags in 1980 and 1981. While volleying sports trivia with players one night, a question asked for the site of John Stockton's first basketball camp. Hill, who grew up and played basketball at tiny Freeman High south of the Spokane Valley, knew the answer. The camp was at Post Falls (Idaho) High. The reason was that Hugh Hobus was the coach there and he helped set it up.

"I knew the answer but they thought I was making it up," Hill said. "And everybody started calling me 'Hobus.' Now, nobody knows my real name. There's still a lot of people who are confused by it."

Zach Gourde: Unsung Zags

Aaron Hill, manager for the Zags during their Elite Eight run in 1999, claimed that one of the untold stories of that group was the effect of its closeness: "We had 14 or 15 guys who hung out together all the time," he said.

But players from that team have pointed in the other direction, and noted that it was Hill, or "Hobus," as he was called, who may have been the mortar to their bricks.

"A guy who really held the program together was Aaron Hill," Zach Gourde said. "He ran the show. By the time he was done, he was in charge on the road. He was so on the ball that they were able to delegate so much responsibility to him that he was in charge of the program in a lot of ways. Lucas Rae was the same way. Those guys were so important in making things run smoothly."

Manager/Bartenders

It's become a customary job share, although it's uncertain how proficiency at one adds to the profitability of the other.

"The last couple managers have followed the same sort of track to survive," Lucas Rae said. "We'd be managers at GU and then work as bartenders at Jack and Dan's [Tavern]. That's kind of become the nature of the job."

When Aaron Hill was hired by Jack and Dan's, co-owner Jack Stockton told him: "Well, this will complete your formal education."

It did.

"Jack and Dan's is the greatest place, everyone is super friendly," Rae said. "But a bar is a bar and sometimes you had to deal with belligerent drunks. One time I had to split up these two guys, one of them was about 6-6, 250, and the other was 6-3, 200 or so, and here I am, six-foot, 175."

Rae looked around for help, saw none, and then just employed a move he might use when mismatched on the baseline against an oversized power forward: "I got between them and put my head down and just started pushing one of them out the door."

Mostly, the lessons were social, not physical.

"The things you learn about how to deal with people are terrific," Hill said. "And the contacts you make in a town like Spokane are so important. Working there was really great."

And it beat laundering sweaty gym shorts all night long.

Mark Few: Unsung Zags

Mentally sifting through Gonzaga success stories, coach Mark Few veered off the conventional story line of walk-on-makes-good and identified a few who surely remained unknown to all but the most fervent fans.

"Lucas Rae was a great Zag story," Few said. "He started out as assistant to the assistant manager and by working hard and being really sharp, he got more and more responsibilities thrown at him. He started out picking up towels and the whole deal, and we were able to put more and more on his shoulders."

Hustling, studying, being responsible, Rae advanced from low manager on the food chain to a job as a full-time assistant coach at Emporia State.

From Manager to Coach

Lucas Rae was a talented enough basketball player to compete at Skagit Valley Community College. He considered walking on at Gonzaga, trying to be one of those guys who overcomes the odds and earns a spot on the roster. After making a realistic evaluation of his chances, he decided against it.

But he still managed to become a critical cog in the team's progression, enough so that he ended up as an assistant coach at Emporia State in Kansas.

"I started out as a student manager and then it kind of evolved into an administrative position," Rae said. "I used to take care of the equipment and do the dirty work; handing out water, picking up towels, doing the laundry."

For endless hours, sometimes through the night, Rae sat in the laundry room, monitoring the clothes, doing his homework.

"It was a good time to get schoolwork done," Rae said. "Nobody was in there and it was quiet."

He studied the game as he worked, too, watching the Gonzaga staff, learning the coaches' approach.

"I'm very lucky, very blessed, to have made this progression," Rae said. "I think if you know basketball, you know basketball. The key to so many things is getting your foot in the door, getting your start, and then just working so hard that they want you to do more things. A good work ethic can take you a long way."

As a college coach, he no longer has to do the team's laundry.

Nor tend bar and break up fights.

Dickau's Dating Service

Further proof that no segregation exists between managers and players at Gonzaga, manager Lucas Rae was good friends with a trio of players—Dan Dickau, Richard Fox and Kyle Bankhead—who lived together in an apartment.

When Rae visited to play cards one time, a co-ed from across the hall just happened to be in attendance. Debate exists whether the set-up was intentional, but she ended up marrying Rae in the summer of 2004.

So, as far as Rae's marriage is concerned, Dickau gets another assist.

CHAPTER EIGHTEEN

From the Land Down Under

Crocodile Dunk-dee

After saving up money at his job flipping burgers at home in Toowoomba, Australia, John Rillie paid his own fare to America and started sampling state-side basketball at Tacoma Community College.

His noted perimeter range had drawn the interest of the Gonzaga staff, of course, especially head coach Dan Fitzgerald, who liked the looks of the slender Aussie. But assistants Dan Monson and Mark Few weren't quite as sold on Rillie as an athlete who could contribute at GU.

"Few came over and watched me work out, and I felt I performed pretty well, making an array of shots," Rillie said in the fall of 2004 as he prepared for another season in the Australia pro league, playing for the Townsville Crocodiles. "The last thing I did was give him my best dunk. As fans in The Kennel would later learn, that's not my forte."

Rillie described a feeble attempt with running start and a one-handed stab that barely went in.

*John Rillie, the bald Australian, was better known for his
long-range jump shots than his drives to the basket.*

"It was really unimpressive," he said. "Back then, the movement
in college was toward the quicker guard who could penetrate and
go to the basket. Here I was, maybe 150 pounds with a somewhat
decent jump shot. I figured right then I better start looking for a
Division II program to go to."

They were right about his dunking. Rillie estimates he made only
two dunks in his three seasons at GU. But he netted a school-record
230 three-pointers in that span, the point equivalent to 345 dunks.

Dirt Sandwiches

Roommate David Cole didn't care how many three-point baskets John Rillie made, he wasn't about to emulate the Australian's diet in an attempt to discover any gastronomic connection to his shooting skills.

"John weighed only about 160 pounds and he used to eat this stuff—Vegemite—that his parents would send him from Australia," Cole said. "The first time we saw that we asked, 'What the hell are you eating?' It looked like dirt; he used to put it on bread and couldn't get enough of it. He talked about it all the time. He just loved it. But that stuff stunk so bad. Man, it was disgusting."

King (Gym) Rat

Generations of insomniac Zags have found their way to the court for late-night or all-night practice sessions. Stockton, Frahm, and countless others—lately Derek Raivio—have all had keys or figured alternate means of entry to accommodate their nocturnal hoop addictions.

John Rillie was different to a degree. It wasn't just practice that was important to Rillie, it was the competition. Competition at any level, in fact. Rillie was seen riding his bike dozens of miles to find a pick-up game. He learned the public transportation schedules as they serviced every cracker-box gym in the region.

"If I heard about a game somewhere, I tried to get there however I could," Rillie said. "Day or night. Bike, bus, or if I could coax somebody into trusting me behind the wheel of their car. I guess you could call it being young and enthusiastic. I was fortunate enough to have a key to the gym at school and I ended up having a good rapport with the night security guys ... good ol' Smitty and the boys."

Coach Dan Fitzgerald loved the single-minded verve, of course, although he used to tease Rillie.

"It's not very politically correct to say it," Rillie said. "But one time he asked me, 'Hey, what were you doing today when you should have been in class ... playing in a pickup game with the five Asian guys wearing brown socks?'"

Fitzgerald took it very seriously once, though, when his prized perimeter threat showed up with a nasty shiner.

"I was playing with some locals over at an east side recreational center and one of the guys busted my eye open pretty well," Rillie said. "It was maybe the day before regular practices were supposed to start, and when Fitz saw the damage, he told me that if he heard of me playing anywhere else outside The Kennel he would fine me a thousand dollars."

Rillie Raining Threes

John Rillie was so hot, so dialed in, that his teammates were leery about even speaking to him, fearful they might disrupt the delicate calibration of his shooting mechanism.

It was in Santa Clara, at the West Coast Conference Tournament in the spring of 1995, and Rillie's uncanny jump shooting had led the Zags into the title game of the tournament against Portland. A berth in the NCAA Tournament went to the winner.

Portland was aligned to defend Rillie, to double him every time he got the ball, to bump him, to jostle him, to beat him to his favored shooting spots. But Rillie just backed up a step or two and continued to shoot over the Pilots.

In the title game, he made eight of 12 shots and all 12 of his free throws for 34 points, setting a tournament record for scoring with 96 points in three games. In that three-game state of unconsciousness, Rillie sank 20 of 28 3-point attempts.

"When you get involved in so many games and practice so hard, it eventually pays off," Rillie explained. "And for me, that was a great time for it all to come together. You've heard people say that when they're really going well, it seems like the game is being played in slow motion. That really was what it was like. Everything felt like I had so much time."

At the time, he was appropriately delighted with the tournament MVP honor and the NCAA berth. But he didn't fully comprehend the historical significance, the way in which his shooting lifted the Zags to their first ever NCAA Tournament appearance.

"In all honesty, I was just so happy to be playing Division I basketball in the U.S., that I was pretty oblivious to a lot of the stuff that was going on," he said. "I watch the NCAAs now and see all of Gonzaga's success and I'm far more emotionally attached to it now than I was when I was playing. I was so wet behind the ears I didn't know what was going on. I was like that puppy in the window just waiting for somebody to pick me up and take me somewhere."

Well, somebody took him to the NCAA Tournament, a destination to which previous Zags had never ventured.

Bald Is Beautiful

Teammates gasped one day when John Rillie showed up with his head cleanly shaved. No sun had reached that scalp for months. Extremely Caucasian and painfully thin, the bald Rillie at first resembled a giant Q-tip.

It made him an easy target for hecklers.

"Many Americans apparently found it very funny," Rillie said. "I won't say [the heckling] fired me up, but the more you're involved in the atmosphere of the game, it makes you concentrate more to put on a top performance for them. I appreciated it; I looked at it as a sign of respect in a way."

Rillie said he always wanted to shave his head, and he and his roommates Kevin Williams and David Cole made a pact to do it late one night. Rillie swears there was no alcohol involved in the shearing process.

"It was one of those late-night things you do in college," Rillie said. "Kevin and I went through with it, but David let us down again. He apparently didn't have the level of testosterone going that we did."

Rillie said that coach Dan Fitzgerald seemed to appreciate the shiny scalp on nights when his shot was falling. "But when I was cold, he'd be like, 'Hey, get that cue ball out of there.'"

Flounder at Guard, Blutarski at Center

When you grow up in Toowoomba, Australia, one's expectations of American college life are shaped by images in movies. And the lifestyle at Gonzaga didn't disappoint John Rillie.

"That group [seniors in 1994] definitely defined what the world perceives as college athletes," Rillie said. "They were all for a good time. When you're an international student and you grow up watching movies, you get this picture in your head of what college life might be about in America. I was just happy to be in America playing basketball, so I was oblivious to a lot of what was going on, but there were sure some times when I could have made some home movies and sold them to friends back home."

What, depravity of the *Animal House* variety? (A new low, we're so ashamed.)

"I won't go that far," Rillie said. "But they were very entertaining at the least."

Rillie marveled, though, that the group did so well on the court, in school, and later in life.

"Those are all successful guys, they all stayed close and all got degrees," he said. "They had a good time, but they also achieved a lot."

Zag World

The Australian Branch of the Gonzaga University Alumni Association could have met in Athens, Greece, in August of 2004.

A sizable portion of the group was on the roster of the Australian Olympic men's basketball team.

Former Zags John Rillie and Paul Rogers both represented their native land.

After a preliminary-round game, the two recalled their experience in America, and neither was totally surprised how the program had attained national acclaim after they finished up in the mid-1990s.

"When you look back, you see that the foundation was there," Rillie said. "There was a lot of hard work put in during those years and people are reaping the rewards now."

Rogers, a seven-foot center with some perimeter skills, claims that the quality of the coaching is at the root of the program's development.

"The building blocks were always there for them; the big thing about the success is the pedigree of the coaches they've had," Rogers said, listing Dan Fitzgerald, Dan Monson, Mark Few and Bill Grier. "Those guys certainly helped me as a big guy develop into an inside player. The fact that I'm still playing now can be attributed to the coaching they gave me when I was there."

As a skilled big man, Rogers was drafted by the Los Angeles Lakers but didn't stick. He's played in a number of international leagues and once spent a season with the Toronto Raptors, although he was on the injured-reserve list the entire year with a broken ankle.

Rillie broke into the Australian pro league as Rookie of the Year and spent six years with the West Sydney Razorbacks, for whom he established several career records. In the fall of 2004, he was playing with the Townsville Crocodiles, where he was a teammate of fellow Zag alum Casey Calvary.

Rillie joined the national team in 2001. Rogers represented Australia in the 2000 Games in Sydney, but said he had to get himself built up and become more physical to make the 2004 team.

The two mostly served as reserves on the Aussie national team. They were roommates on the road, and spent considerable time talking about the days at Gonzaga.

Both were delighted, without a hint of jealousy, over the success and attention the contemporary Zags enjoy.

"Oh, no, mate, somebody has to start it all off," Rillie said. "I'm glad it was us."

John Rillie: Being a Zag

Assimilation into a new culture in a different hemisphere takes time. For John Rillie, the focus of his life in America was the same as it was Down Under: Playing basketball. It allowed him to fit in quickly with his new teammates and friends.

"It just seems like one big fraternity," Rillie said. "That is the unique experience going to that school. The basketball guys all keep in contact with their former teammates because there's a special bond that comes with it. When you talk to guys who went to other schools, there doesn't seem to be the same relationship and rapport once you all go your separate ways."

Zag Myth: Recumbent Rillie Nets Three

John Rillie, the Australian Bomber noted for outrageous range with his jump shot, is reputed to have once made a shot from somewhere in the 40- to 45-foot range while SEATED on the Gonzaga bench in pregame warmups.

From that angle, from that distance, with no legs to help power the shot ... some contend the slender Rillie simply could not generate the necessary oomph.

"Yes, Rillie did make a shot sitting on the bench," Scott Snider confirms. "I believe it was before one of the WCC tourney games in 1995 when John carried us to our first NCAA tourney. As is customary for John, he would take one shot in warmups and sit on our team bench. This is the pre-pregame warmups [45 minutes until tip]. I would usually sit with him after I shot once or twice.

"John and I would sit down and the only time we would move is when a ball would roll over to the bench. John picked up a ball and shot it. Sure enough he swished it. After that moment, I knew he was feeling it."

From Australia, Rillie confirmed the shot. Except it turns out that it happened more than once. He also made one at home before a game.

"Most guys go and shoot around to hone their skills," Rillie said. "I think that if you practice a lot during the week, those 20 minutes are worthless and you're probably playing more mind games with yourself. One day I was over there where the Kennel Club comes in, sitting down, and I lobbed one in."

How far? 40 feet? 45? "Yeah, probably."

Sitting down? No legs?

"Yeah," he said. "And they always complained I didn't do enough weight lifting, and that I wasn't strong enough."

Zag Quip

Coach Dan Fitzgerald's insightful and complex strategic advice to his team before the 1995 West Coast Conference Tournament, when sharp-shooting, shaved-headed, gunner-from-down-under John Rillie was on a streak when he couldn't miss from deep:

"Get the round thing to the bald thing."

CHAPTER NINETEEN

Frozen Tundra

Frozen Few

Make back-to-back Elite Eight and Sweet 16 appearances, and fans don't expect you to start losing to Boise State and Wisconsin-Green Bay. So, when the 2000-2001 season was mired in a December swoon, pressure began building.

Boise State absolutely owned the Zags, 94-69, in a loss that coach Mark Few absorbed with particular personal pain, considering his Boise-native in-laws were on hand to witness the bludgeoning.

They then lost by 14 at Florida before completing a meteorologically challenging trek to Green Bay. The temperature swing was nearly 100 degrees, and the Zags' shooting reflected the chill.

"It was just an accumulation of your worst moments," Few said. "We were just plain awful; we weren't ready and we had that look you get on the road sometimes when you're lethargic. And the home team was fired up, of course."

Guard Dan Dickau, a steadying force in such situations, was out with an injury he suffered in the loss to Arizona, and the Zags were left vulnerable in his absence.

Few approached the locker room at halftime ready to blister the paint off the walls with a well-timed excoriation of his withering troops. But he'd barely made it into the hallway when he heard another voice already tearing them apart, using the same ferocity, heck, even some of the same words, Few had expected to unleash.

"Mark Spink gave quite a halftime talk," Few said. "I was going to lay into them, but I could hear Spink rattling the walls from outside the locker room. As bad as that whole thing was, it was one of my prouder moments because he was saying exactly what I would have been saying as a head coach."

Despite Spink's extensive vocabulary of challenging insults, the Zags still fell 72-61 to sit at 5-4 with a long trip home and a lengthy break in the schedule ahead of them.

Few needed to clear his head, and shake out the swirling visions of his program in a steep tailspin. So, wearing his suit and dress shoes—no overcoat—he decided to walk back to the hotel.

The National Weather Service archives report that the low temperature on December 20, 2000 was minus-5 degrees. The wind was steady at 15 miles per hour, with gusts up to 20 miles per hour. Wind chill tables show that combination to feel like the biting equivalent of 30 degrees below zero.

The heat from the frustration-induced and internally generated steam soon dissipated, and Few began feeling the helplessness of the Dallas Cowboys' defensive line in the famous Ice Bowl at Lambeau Field.

"I thought you could see the hotel from the arena, and I wanted to get off by myself," Few said. "It was one of those things where you take off and get about halfway into something and then you go, 'Hmm, this wasn't such a good move.'"

Few tried to cut across an open area, but a deep snowbank blocked his path.

His mind had been filled with the dread that his team had hit rock bottom, and that they'd struggle to win another game. And, suddenly, those fears were replaced by another: That he'd be frozen somewhere in the neighborhood of Lambeau Field and he wouldn't be found until the spring thaw.

"But it was," Few said, "a good way to clear my head."

Blizzard of Doubts

The pressure early in the 2000-2001 season to match the previous year's success escalated to red-line levels when the preconference record fell to 5-4. Losses at Arizona (after a Dan Dickau injury) and Florida carried no disgrace, but the Zags fell in a "Crusade Game" at Boise State (the kind where an opponent's win causes fans to storm the court), and then executed an absolute face plant into the snow at Wisconsin-Green Bay.

Against a packed-in zone, the Zags shot poorly and lost to a team they'd defeated by 27 points at home earlier in the season. One year after making it to the Sweet 16, the Zags found themselves barely above .500.

"After the game, Mark takes off in this snowstorm and walks back to the hotel in just his suit ... no overcoat," Leon Rice recalled. His anger had hardly abated when he called Leon Rice and Bill Grier together during a layover on the flight home.

"He said, 'Fellas, we've got to do a better job or we're going to be known as the guys who ran the Gonzaga program into the ground,'" Rice said.

Grier and Rice had no trouble interpreting Few's message, and neither did the team, which had been likewise blistered by Few. Suitably inspired, the Zags raced through the West Coast Conference season with a 13-1 record and again advanced to the Sweet 16 before falling to Michigan State.

As the wins stacked up and the rankings elevated, Rice and Grier sometimes check the standings and the polls, and can't help but needle each other.

"We'll say, 'Yep, we're going to be known as the guys who ran this program into the ground,'" Rice said. "Mark doesn't know we joke about it."

He does now.

Turning Point: A Green Bay Tavern

The Green Bay loss spawned self-examination by more Zags than just coach Mark Few. And the results of this introspection would revive the season.

"I remember Casey Calvary and Mark Spink taking off after that game, disappearing to one of the bars," Zach Gourde recalled. "Drinking was not the order of business; they went off to take personal inventory."

Calvary and Spink were the two strongest players on the team; Calvary with his physical nature and intensity, Spink with his leadership and intellect.

"They were our captains and our leaders," Gourde said. "And the two of them really took the initiative that night to make sure they knew what our goals were, where the Zag spirit was, where it had gone, and how we could best go about getting it back. Those two were critical in getting us turned around; they really changed the direction our team was going after that."

"Coach Few was livid; he hated us, and rightly so," Spink said. "We found a bar close to the hotel and just sat there and put tears in our beers. Casey and I had been to the Elite Eight and the Sweet 16, and now we were seniors and it was on our shoulders and it was going to hell."

Calvary and Spink had been among those who had elevated the program to national recognition, and a loss in Green Bay, to any team that wasn't the Packers, was simply an unacceptable development.

The fear, in Spink's mind, at least, was that the Zags who followed his group had known nothing but success and might be unaware of the kind of work and attitude it took to reach that level in the first place.

"At that point, we had started to get some big-time recruits like Blake Stepp and Cory Violette," Spink said. "They were great guys, but we were worried that we had guys who came in thinking

Gonzaga, oh, this is a big-time program and all you have to do is show up and win games.

"Casey and I were from the old guard who got the crap beat out of us as freshmen and sophomores. We didn't want guys who were there to ride the wave and not really understand what Gonzaga basketball stood for. From that point, we had to let the fellas know that you can't take anything for granted and you can't just show up and win games."

And in a rare statement to arise after a night in a Green Bay tavern, Spink assessed that night as "a very sobering experience."

Cheeseheads for a Day

Trainer Steve DeLong and assistant coach Scott Snider, holed up in a Green Bay hotel with a day to kill before a game against Wisconsin-Green Bay, heard an interesting come-on from the evening news. The Packers were to play host to Tampa Bay in a critical game at Lambeau Field, and fans were invited to come to the stadium to shovel tons of snow off the stands.

The pay was six dollars per hour. DeLong, Snider and manager Aaron Hill took off at 7 a.m. intending to help defrost the Frozen Tundra.

"It was pretty damned cold," said Snider, who had mooched sweatshirts and gloves from team members. They were handed shovels and pointed toward the stands. Some 150 fans were busily at work.

"Several times, fans would start 'Go Packers' chants and start cussing out Tampa Bay fans," Snider said.

The novelty wore off quickly, Snider noted, and the Zag representatives turned in their shovels after an hour and a half, pocketed their $9 each, and walked back to the hotel.

CHAPTER TWENTY

Myths, McPhee, Big Mons

Zag Myth: Bartender Joins Team

Yes, coaches Dan Monson and Mark Few bolstered the Gonzaga front line with a big man who was tending bar at the Outback Tavern in Spokane.

Actually, it was more a case of luring Martin Dioli back onto the roster after he had given up the sport for a year.

"It was a busy Friday or Saturday night and I was working behind the bar," recalled Dioli, a San Francisco attorney who evidently passed two different kinds of bar exams. "I look up and there's Dan Monson and Mark Few. I made a crack about them wanting a round on the house. They said something to the effect of, 'Do you want to come back and play basketball?' I didn't even think about it, I said, 'Sure, yeah, I do.'"

As Dioli recalls, the Zags had lost a junior college big man they thought they were going to get, and a couple guys had left the team. Monson, Few and coach Dan Fitzgerald kicked around ideas on what to do when they remembered that Dioli still had eligibility remaining, although he hadn't played in more than a year.

"I had already graduated and was just tending bar and studying for my [Law School Aptitude Test]," said Dioli, whose weight had risen from the 245-pound displacement during his playing days to a robust bartenderly 275.

He rejoined the team for the 1991 season and was thankful for the opportunity at a second chance.

"I always regretted the decision to not play that year," he said. "I had never quit anything and I always knew you shouldn't quit something you've committed to. I really missed my teammates and the camaraderie and the experience. I'm thankful they asked me back."

Dioli recalled getting in Fitzgerald's doghouse, earlier, when he was whistled for a couple traveling calls in a game against Pepperdine. "Fitz blew his top and spent the entire halftime yelling at me," Dioli said. "After the game, we were going out and [teammate] Chris Delaney came up and asked if I was okay."

Delaney told him that Fitzgerald had sent him in search of Dioli to make certain he was doing all right after the coach had chewed off a major portion of his ass.

"That's how he was; he'd get really mad and lose his temper, but in the end, you knew he was concerned about you and wanted the best for you. It wasn't malicious, even when he was being really harsh and making you feel like you didn't deserve to live."

Zag Tickets, No Thanks

Jim McPhee just arrived at Gonzaga in the fall of 1986 and was provided an immediate and unmistakable display of how the program was viewed in the region.

As one of the freshman players, he was told to head over to Northtown Mall and distribute schedule posters for the upcoming GU season. The poster, he remembered, bore a picture of coach Dan Fitzgerald wearing a hard hat and proclaimed that "Blue Collar Basketball is Back."

So, the earnest McPhee popped into retailers throughout the mall. "They wouldn't even take it," he said.

Along with the posters, the players tried handing out coupons redeemable for game tickets to the team's first couple contests. They wouldn't take those, either.

"We could not give the tickets away," McPhee said. "Now you can't even buy a ticket."

Literature Appreciation

Jim McPhee, an attorney in Spokane, appreciated that Gonzaga was a program—under coach Dan Fitzgerald—where academics were seriously stressed.

While the NCAA had a certain minimum grade-point average established to govern a player's eligibility, McPhee recalled that Fitzgerald's minimum was considerably higher.

"He always talked about academics coming first," McPhee said. "One time I had this American Literature paper that was due and I wasn't happy with where I was with it. I came to practice and told him that and he immediately said: 'Get out of here.'"

Requiem for Hank

Jim McPhee wished to extend a personal thanks to the Loyola Marymount team under coach Paul Westhead. Of McPhee's 2,015 career points (second most in Gonzaga history), he figured an outrageous percentage came against Westhead's incidental defense. An example was the second meeting of the 1989 season, when LMU allowed the Zags to score 136 points, but nonetheless won the game by 11 points.

At the West Coast Conference Tournament in Los Angeles in March of 1989, McPhee cracked the 2,000-point barrier in the opener against LMU. McPhee had no idea of his point total until he raced back down the court one time to guard prolific scorer Bo Kimble, and Kimble stopped to shake his hand.

LMU dumped the struggling Zags 121-84, but Westhead wanted to honor McPhee's point total by giving him the game ball the next day during their second-round game. McPhee, the consummate student/athlete, politely declined because he had a mid-term exam looming and he needed to study.

The next day, LMU star Hank Gathers collapsed during the game and died of heart problems. McPhee still gets choked up with the recollection.

"That guy was such a warrior," McPhee said of Gathers. "That tournament, we were all in the L.A. Hilton lobby, we were coming back from shootaround and they were on their way to theirs. The lobby was really crowded but Hank made eye contact with us, with this psycho look on his face, and it was game over right then."

Not that he was dangerous; just extremely intense.

"He was a great guy, a really great guy," McPhee said. "But he was such an animal of a competitor. Before the game, he would jump rope at center court and just stare down the guy he was going to play against."

Jim McPhee's All-Time Zag

Having played against Bo Kimble and Hank Gathers, and other stars of the WCC and elsewhere, Jim McPhee has no hesitation when identifying the best player he competed with or against: GU guard Doug Spradley (Zag, '89).

"More than anybody I ever played with or against, he's a guy who deserved to be in the NBA," McPhee said. "He was so talented and so competitive."

Spradley coaches in Germany now, McPhee said. "He's very well-respected over there."

Although, for physical power and toughness, McPhee pinpointed Dale Haaland (Zag, '87), whom he once saw just flatten a giant Boise State center on his way up for a thunder dunk.

Coach Dan Fitzgerald customarily would provide the team with extensive scouting reports of opponents and then quiz the Zags on them before the game. Players had to respond with appropriate and detailed answers whether their man could go to the left, or had range on his jump shot, or liked to drive the baseline.

To fail to respond with a complete and cogent answer meant a trip to Fitz's woodshed.

McPhee remembered a time when Haaland's aggressiveness emerged in Fitzgerald's Socratic pregame session.

"We were playing San Diego and they had a seven-footer named Scott Thompson," McPhee said. "Fitz asked Dale about Thompson, and he simply answered: 'He's a #$%&!'"

Fitzgerald, apparently appreciative of Haaland's poetic brevity, responded: "Okay, let's go get 'em!"

A Lucky Break

Just a good rule of thumb: Don't get between Martin Dioli and a pizza.

Shivering in their hotel rooms in a wickedly cold late December night in Casper, Wyoming, while in town for the 1988 Cowboy Shootout, Martin Dioli, Brian Fredrickson and Paul Verret ordered a pizza. As Dioli remembers it, he and Frederickson started wrestling over who would get the final slice. Verret was out of contention because he had earlier suffered a stress fracture in his lower leg and was reclining on a bed with his crutches.

As the battle for the pizza escalated, the massive Dioli cast Fredrickson in the air, flying, tumbling, floating in space toward Verret.

"He landed right on Paul and turned that stress fracture into a clean break," Dioli said. "But as it turned out, that helped the healing process for some reason. [Trainer] Steve DeLong was really pissed at first, but it turned out to be beneficial."

The Disappearing Marlon Wadlington

Gary Payton's glove-tight defense couldn't shut down Marlon Wadlington. The Gonzaga point guard was having a nice game against Payton and the Oregon State Beavers in December of 1986. At halftime, coach Dan Fitzgerald praised Wadlington's efforts.

"In the second half, though, I didn't play nearly as much as I should have played," said Wadlington, an attorney in Los Angeles. "When we came off the court, Fitz looked at me kind of surprised and said, 'Marlon, where have you been? We needed you in there. You've got to get in my face when I don't put you in the game.'

"I said, 'Coach, I thought that was your job.' He got so amped up about what was going on, he forgot about me."

Gym McPhee

Players and staff universally respected Jim McPhee for his attitude, hustle, scholarship and skills. But his personal hygiene around the basketball floor, whew, that's another matter.

"I have no idea why, but he wore the same shirt through the whole season and oh, my God, did he reek," teammate Marlon Wadlington said. "He never had it washed. About the third week, it would stand stiff in his locker and would stay stiff until he started sweating into it again. It was the worst smelling thing you could imagine."

Fended off aggressive defenders, though.

Marlon Wadlington: Being a Zag

Looking back, "it was the best experience I could have ever had," attorney Marlon Wadlington said of his time at Gonzaga. "It made me grow up. We worked hard, we partied hard, but we had a bond that made it like we were brothers. I have to give Dan Fitzgerald credit for that; he constantly fostered that type of environment. He wanted everybody to be considered a member of the family."

As another very successful professional in his post-Zag days, Wadlington said it was an outgrowth of the atmosphere at GU.

"It is a fine school, and it was always instilled in us that you had to take care of business. We looked at the bigger picture outside of basketball; we were told how to be successful, and the people at Gonzaga created a very supportive environment."

Coaches Emeritus

Some guys retire to Florida or Arizona. Don Monson and Jud Heathcote hung up their whistles and moved in behind the Gonzaga bench.

Together, they bring decades of experience to the arena, and archival knowledge of the game's strategies, tactics and coaching philosophies. All of which the Gonzaga staff eagerly draws upon.

Monson coached at Idaho and Oregon, taking the Vandals to a Sweet 16 appearance. Heathcote, of course, won an NCAA championship with Magic Johnson at Michigan State.

Monson retired to Spokane when his son, Dan, was a GU assistant; Heathcote had been a high school coach in town and liked the environment.

"For a group of young coaches like we were, it's a great resource," Bill Grier said of the two veterans. "Leon [Rice] and I met last fall with Jud to go through some different ideas on our match-up zone [defense]. Just having them to bounce some ideas off and get feedback from is amazing. Their experience is so valuable to us and we always listen to what they have to say."

Mark Few has lunch with Heathcote every week, and visits on the phone in between.

"You get good feedback from them after the games that you might not have picked up on," Few said. "They're never lacking in opinions. What an awesome resource for us to have. They're very important to us."

CHAPTER TWENTY-ONE

On the Road, Etc.

Fender Bender

A car in front of Leon Rice on Interstate 5 stopped abruptly, and Rice had to slam on his brakes. The driver in the car trailing him was not so alert, as he bashed into the rear end of Rice's car, causing some $500 damage.

Rice, making recruiting rounds in the Seattle area, stepped out of the vehicle to survey the damage.

"I was kind of flustered," Rice said. "And this teenage kid who was driving comes up and sees my shirt. He says, 'Gonzaga? I love Gonzaga.'"

The drivers exchanged information, with the promise that the young Gonzaga fan would pay for the repair.

"After he had paid every penny, I sent him a Gonzaga t-shirt," Rice said.

With the prized garment, Rice enclosed this note: "This is the most expensive Gonzaga t-shirt you'll ever buy."

Traveling Violations

Coaches Bill Grier and Jerry Krause kid that they should commission a psychological study of the bus drivers who have ferried the

Zags over the years. "Every one of them has some kind of a quirk, and every one of them drives like a maniac," Grier contended. "We were at the Jimmy V Classic one year and the bus driver was a crazy man, running yellow lights, tailgating, going way too fast. He was following this woman so close that when she stopped for a yellow light, he just bashed right into her."

Police needed to be called to investigate, leaving the team on the side of the road.

"The unbelievable thing was the way he tried to get Jerry to be a witness that the woman was to blame because she didn't run the yellow light."

Leave the Driving to Us

In an approach deemed by some too parsimonious for a Division I program, the Zags used to take buses to their games at Portland instead of flying. It was one of coach Dan Fitzgerald's ideas.

Jim McPhee heard that Portland coach Larry Steele had used that against the Zags during recruiting season. "Steele was the coach and supposedly when we were going after the same kid one time, he said something like: 'You don't want to go to GU, they have to ride buses down here.'"

Fitzgerald could not let that slide, of course.

"We were down there one time and were just killing them," McPhee said. "Fitz looked at Steele and told him, 'We came down here on a bus, we whipped you, and now we're getting back on the bus and going back to Spokane.'"

Shampoo Costs Extra

The trip to Portland back in the 1980s brought an added delight, aside from the lengthy bus ride, alumni director Marty Pujolar recalled.

"We always stayed at a place up off North Burnside called the Courson Arms. It was $10 per night per kid," Pujolar said. "And we put three or four kids in every room."

Any revolts?

"No, nobody knew any better."

Cleanliness Is Next to Zag-liness

Litter and it will cost you. Especially in the Gonzaga basketball locker room.

More than once, an untidy locker room has caused GU coaches to evict the Zags from their cozy cubicles.

"Guys have a tendency to still think their moms are around and are going to pick up their laundry for them and clean up after them," coach Mark Few said. "When it reaches a certain point, we have to toss them out of the locker room."

You mean that these guys—reputed for their classwork and community involvement—aren't the best about policing their area?

"There is no correlation whatsoever between intelligence and good hygiene and pride in their personal space," Few said. "None whatsoever."

Unexpected Nose Job

Bakari Hendrix, the West Coast Conference's 1998 Player of the Year, may have improved as much as any Zag over the course of his career, earning only 34 minutes of playing time as a sophomore only to become the league's top scorer as a senior.

Mark Spink recalls how physical and intense Hendrix was during practice ... reasons for his remarkable advancement, no doubt.

"He was one of those really tough guys who got in fights in practice because he was so tenacious," Spink said. "If guys weren't getting after it, he'd let them know."

In the Zags' second-round NIT game at Hawaii that year, Hendrix accidentally showed a Rainbow player how powerful he was.

"Bakari grabbed a rebound in traffic and turned and just absolutely ripped this guy's nose off his face," Spink said. "Blood everywhere. I was sitting there on the bench going, geez, this is one rugged guy."

Defenders tried grabbing and screaming, but Bakari Hendrix still became the 1998 West Coast Conference Player of the Year.

Marc, They Call Them "Caucasians"

One display of transcendent Zag Pride sticks out in Scott Spink's memory.

At one point during a Gonzaga romp over Saint Mary's, Marc Armstead noted that the Zags had five white players on the floor to Saint Mary's five blacks.

Armstead, an African-American, felt it worthy of a comment to his opponents.

"I'll never forget it," Spink said. "Marc starts yelling at the Saint Mary's huddle: 'These white guys are kicking your ass.'"

The Best Zag Nobody Knew: Felix McGowan

Felix McGowan (Zag, '93) came out of junior college ready to wow Gonzaga fans. But they rarely got a chance to see him. His teammates, though, saw plenty.

"He was going to be the next great guard," Scott Spink said. "He had all the skills and talent of anyone I had ever seen. He could run and jump and shoot. He was a jaycee guy, so he only had two years, and in his first year, he backed up Jarrod Davis, who almost never came out, and in his senior year, he broke his hand in our first league game. Fitz put in this bald-headed kid from Australia [John Rillie] and everybody knows the rest."

Tight Quarters, Close Team

Before moving into the new arena, the Gonzaga coaches' offices occupied small spaces on a small campus. The team and staff stayed close, since no other option was available. The offices had windows that looked out on the court, and were only two flights of stairs above the locker rooms and training room.

"That's one of the neat things about here," coach Bill Grier said. "Our guys are in our offices every day. We get real interaction with every one of them every day."

As he spoke, center Ronny Turiaf walked past, peaked in, and updated him on his schedule.

"I know it's one of the things that Dan [Monson] misses at Minnesota," Grier said. "It's all so spread out there, that he doesn't get as much interaction with the players outside of practice."

From Maitre'd to UCLA

When Ben Howland was hired from Pittsburgh to take over the storied UCLA basketball program, former GU coach Dan Fitzgerald remembered the ignominious manner in which Howland started his coaching career at Gonzaga.

Howland took a non-paying job as a grad assistant with the Zags under coach Jay Hillock. And Ben and his wife, Kim, lived in a small apartment across the Spokane River from the school.

Fitzgerald, then the athletic director, wanted to help the Howlands make ends meet. He phoned a friend over at Playfair Race Course to see if somebody could help provide part-time employment for Howland.

"Does he own a tie?" Fitzgerald was asked.

Yes.

"Good, we'll make him the host at the Turf Club [restaurant]," the friend said. "He can greet and seat the visitors."

So, Howland's first criterion for employment on the way up to the prestigious UCLA job was ownership of suitable neckwear.

Fitzgerald kidded him that it could have been much worse.

"Some of the baseball guys used to have to help the veterinarians collect horse [urine] for the post-race drug samples."

Best Zag Never to Play?

Assistant coach Tommy Lloyd remembers spending most of one season as a nanny to prospective Zag player Mario Kasun. The effort seemed worth it at the time, as the Croatian sensation was seven-foot-one and 260 pounds.

"He had a bunch of eligibility issues and was never able to play because he had an affiliation with a pro club over there," Lloyd said. "The NCAA gave us all kinds of hang-ups, but when he left, then the NCAA changed the rule."

Eventually, Kasun was drafted in the second round in 2002 by the Los Angeles Clippers. In the fall of 2004, his rights had been traded to the Orlando Magic, who provided him with a guaranteed contract.

"He may have been the most talented kid ever to come through here," Lloyd said. "He's 7-1, runs like a deer, handles the ball and shoots threes. But I think I spent the whole year monitoring Mario, trying to get him to class, trying to get him up, you name it. He was a good, funloving kid, always laughing and smiling, but getting him to be a student was like pulling teeth."

He was colorful, too, as his epidermis displayed.

"He's got tattoos everywhere," Lloyd said. "His family was very poor, but one time they sent him over $70 and I remember he took $35 and went and got his eyebrow pierced."

The Dreaded 10-miler

The challenge occupied an unsettled place in their minds all summer. Before players took an extra dessert or washed it down with a brew, they thought about the 10-mile run that was looming ahead of them.

For a time, coach Dan Fitzgerald force marched his troops in an annual 10-mile run at the start of their training camp. It was a test of their fitness, but also an incentive for them to spend the summers working out rather than growing soft. The standard for big men was 80 minutes, and for the smaller guys, 70 minutes.

One exhausted player, Lango Taylor (Zag, '92), entered GU lore by deliriously starting to strip off his clothes and throwing his shoes in the Spokane River.

In the fall of 1989, Zag Michael Storm fell far behind the pack, and Fitzgerald and Monson hopped in a car to go find him.

"We thought we lost him," Monson said. "We found him at about seven miles and Fitz drove up next to him and lowered the window. Storm tried grabbing the door like he was going to get in and ride the rest of the way. Fitz screamed, 'What the $%^&# are you doing? I'm not here to give you a ride; I'm here to chew your ass. Get to that finish line ... NOW ... you're 10 minutes behind.'

"Fitz then sped off," Monson said. "He almost ripped Storm's hand off the door as he was trying to climb in."

Husky Refugees

Defectors from the University of Washington have created a rich legacy of basketball success following transfer to Gonzaga. Not to suggest that the in-state big brother actually serves as a minor-league feeder program, but Eric Brady, Jeff Brown, Jason Bond, Dan Dickau and Erroll Knight all flourished after giving up Seattle in favor of Spokane.

Brown went on to become the West Coast Conference Player of the Year and national scholar athlete; Dickau was an Associated Press first-team All-American.

The story is told that former Zags coach Dan Fitzgerald once asked UW coach Lynn Nance if his team had its media guide ready yet, because he needed to have a look at it.

The curious Nance pushed Fitzgerald for a reason. Fitz kidded: "I want to start scouting who we're going to get from you next year."

Hey, He Was There for a While

Is the Washington program envious of the success of those players who emigrated to Gonzaga?

In the UW media guide under "Huskies In The Pros," you'll find the name "Dan Dickau."

And You Dated Cindy Crawford, Too

Pepperdine had just clobbered the Zags of 1991 in Malibu, which wasn't unexpected. The Waves were dominant in the West

Coast Conference at the time. That didn't mean the Zags couldn't have some fun with a teammate's misfortune.

"We got railed by Pep and we were loading a minivan when Rob Rich went to throw a bag in the back and hit his head on the tailgate," Jarrod Davis said. "He split his head wide open and was gushing blood. Steve DeLong was there to doctor him, but he got, literally, temporary amnesia."

Ah, amnesia ... the comic possibilities.

"On the ride back to the hotel from Malibu we told him that we had smoked Pepperdine and he had 30 points and eight dunks," Davis said. "And as the story got rolling, we just kept making it bigger and bigger. He ate it up."

Zags in Transition

Old Zags see the difference. They weren't on national television or in the rankings. But they have reason to be proud of what they accomplished and how it helped lay the foundation of later success.

"It's changed," Jarrod Davis said. "The guys before us were hard-nosed guys who played their asses off but maybe lacked a bit of talent. My years, it started to change a little bit, with guys who still busted their butts but had some talent."

Some of the difference, Davis concedes, was in attitude and expectation.

"We just had guys who had so much fun being together; now, there's been so much success, that they're so much more serious. A lot of the guys now don't even drink or stay out. For us, we were all about how late you could stay out and how many girls you could hook up with. So, it's changed from when I played. But it's been a unique transition."

CHAPTER TWENTY-TWO

Zag Effort

Hertz's Hat Trick

It's another unseen tradition for the Zags, the way former baseball coach Steve Hertz, now the director of athletic relations, appears in the locker room after games to present a ball cap to the player he feels best displayed "Zag Effort."

Late in the Zags' difficult 8-20 season of 1989-90, Dan Fitzgerald asked Hertz to give a talk. The team won. And they won again the next time he did it. Ever since, Hertz hasn't missed his postgame ball cap presentation.

"I told them I didn't know diddly about basketball," Hertz said. "But I know about effort and I know about being a Zag."

Hertz doesn't target just the high scorer or the statistically dominant player.

"Sometimes it might be a redshirt on the bench," he said. "Sometimes the trainer got the award, or an assistant who did the scouting for the game."

Sometimes, Hertz will poll assistant coaches for a player who might need a boost. Other times, Hertz lays into them if he doesn't see the kind of effort he's come to expect.

"They can't go out there and dog it because they know I'll come in and say, 'What the hell was that? You've got to be kidding me.'"

Hertz has performed the service under the guidance of three different head coaches, and whenever there's been a change, he's checked to be certain he was still wanted. Every year, he's invited back. And while he's giving the award, Hertz said that he's the one feeling rewarded.

"It's an honor I dearly love," Hertz said. "It goes deeper than my capacity to express it."

A Personal Presentation

Gonzaga players Zach Gourde and Winston Brooks had heard that Steve Hertz's daughter, Heather, was about to start radiation in an attempt to fend off cancer. They invited her into the locker room for the "hat" ceremony, hoping it would lift her spirits.

"It was really an inspirational moment for her," Hertz said. "Zach told her how sure he was she was going to beat this and that everybody in that room was behind her. It meant so much to her."

The next morning, Hertz received a letter under his office door from Brooks, telling him how much Heather's courage had inspired him.

"A lot of people may not know much about Winston from his play, but he was a giant in that program," Hertz said. "To this day, if he ever needed me for anything ... I will be there. He is a guy who, on top of playing and going to school, used to coach an AAU team of 11- and 12-year-olds who were throw-offs from other teams. And he was a guardian for his two younger brothers at the time, like a dad to them. That's the kind of guy Winston Brooks is."

And Heather?

"She's doing great," Hertz said. "We're winning that game."

Steve Hertz: Being a Zag

The level of attention and frequency of victories have changed. But at the core, the basketball is much the same.

"Going back to when I started coaching here in the late 1970s, actually, even before that, when I was an athlete here, the character of the people who have played basketball here has never changed. I see the same fight, the same great efforts, the same quality coaching, and almost the same process.

"When you boil it down to look at a couple key players, the inspiration came from Stockton, and Jeff Brown's transfer really ignited it. It used to feel like we had these great things going on, but it was off-Broadway. It was well done and well respected, but it wasn't that well known.

"I know that with all the alums I deal with, they're all elated that this thing has hit it big now. What this program has accomplished has been absolutely *Twilight Zone* scary. But what is amazing, and it's kind of corny, but it's been done the Zag way. There's something special about it, and now it's just a matter of it being a hit ON-Broadway where people now can see what Zags are all about."

Zags Sing Crosby

Montana was always an inhospitable venue for the Zags. But during a holiday tournament in December 1980, GU had a breakthrough that left the Zags singing like a mesomorphic glee club.

"We got 19 wins that year and had a great run in the league," said Ken Anderson, now a professor in the Gonzaga School of Business and the university's faculty representative to the NCAA. "We absolutely put the hurt on Murray State in the first game and had a hellacious game with Montana in the championship. Donny Baldwin, the best guy I played with here, nailed a jumper with three seconds left to win it."

When the trophies were handed out, the MVP honors went to a Grizzly guard, instead of Baldwin, probably less out of provincialism than the fact that voting on these things always takes place well before the game's final minutes.

"[Coach Dan Fitzgerald] went nuts about that, screaming how Baldwin got screwed," Anderson said.

Still, it was a pair of nice wins in a tough venue ... a memorable moment, eh?

"The single most memorable moment for me as a Zag," Anderson said. "Came that night when we all went to the Stockman's Bar. Everybody was there, including the young freshman point guard [John Stockton]. And we're in their bar, after having won their tournament, singing every Bing Crosby song we could think of. It was the greatest time."

This, Anderson feels, was more than just a close group of guys gathering to slur old songs on a sudsy night in Montana. This was an early step toward something that could develop at Gonzaga.

"This was a special time; we were legit," Anderson said. "The previous year had a little bit of a renegade feel to it. We were part of a new trend. Fitz had to decide which way he was going to take the program, scrambling to put a team together. But we were a solid group of guys who also put together a real nice season.

"Fitz didn't have to worry about us not working hard; he had to worry about us not beating the shit out of each other," Anderson said. "That 'play hard, play smart' idea was just a saying, but we did it ... we made that a permanent part of the program."

No Bull

It was, Ken Anderson stressed, a different era. Players would drive the rental cars on the road and be just about as "social" as was possible and still make it to the games for tip off.

"We had Saint Mary's coming in one Thursday, and on Wednesday night, there was a party bus that went out to a bar in Hayden Lake called Gator McClusky's," Anderson said. "I remember feeling that I showed pretty good restraint ... I didn't ride the mechanical bull. That was my idea of restraint because we were playing the next night."

That team won 19 games, and may have established a school record for partying, held at least until the 1994 class mounted a serious challenge to the title.

"I couldn't imagine having a better time," Anderson said. "We didn't worry too much about what we did. In that regard, we were really lucky nothing ever happened. In those days, you just didn't have all the oversight and concern over certain issues on campus they do now."

Anderson was among a group that could play hard, do well in school and party with the same determined intensity.

"Fitz liked that we could do well in our classes and play our asses off but didn't think we were very good role models for the younger guys because he didn't want them seeing us staying out until three a.m. because not everybody can do that," Anderson said.

The conference race that season came down to an overtime loss to Portland in Spokane. But it wasn't all disappointment for that cluster of Zags.

"I can't imagine having a better time than we had," Anderson said.

Even without the mechanical bull ride.

The Grateful Graduate

On the day Lorenzo Rollins graduated from Gonzaga University, he dressed in the ceremonial cap and gown at 8 a.m., wore it proudly the entire day, and only with reluctance did he finally remove them. They were, after all, vestments symbolic of Rollins's considerable journey.

The GU basketball program had pulled off many unlikely achievements, but none of the upsets might have been as stunning— or have said so much about the values of the program—as Rollins's collection of a diploma that day.

"That was the greatest accomplishment of my life," said Rollins (Zag, '97). "To get that degree, in front of my family ... "

Nobody questioned that the sinewy six-foot-five guard with the silky shot and fluid game would contribute to the Zag teams. His range and facility for scoring made that a certainty. But most would have wagered heavily on the "under" if his graduation prospects had been placed on the Vegas boards.

Classified as an academic "non-predictor" out of Tacoma's Foss High, the highly recruited Rollins put in two years at Tacoma Community College and was—after fervent vouching by coaches—given a chance at Gonzaga.

"That's one of the real success stories of the program," Dan Fitzgerald, former GU head coach, later said. "You hear a lot about the bad things about college athletics, well, he's a walking ad for why you give scholarships. This guy sacrificed, disciplined himself to get to class, and had about as drastic social adjustment as you can have to deal with. The guy who deserves credit for Lorenzo Rollins getting a degree is Lorenzo Rollins. Yeah, we stayed on his ass, but this guy earned it."

The steadying and loving influence of his mother always shepherded Rollins, but he still was exposed to youthful drug deals and the spray of vagrant bullets. Along with engaging in the personal quest of elevating his game, Rollins's efforts also were diverted to the earnest chore of keeping his chalk outline off some slab of Tacoma pavement. Frankly, these were not the experiences of his typical Gonzaga classmates.

Coach Mark Few, then an assistant to Fitzgerald, believed in Rollins and urged everyone to take a chance on him.

"He's really a sweetheart of a kid, and his mother's a terrific person," Few said at the time. "He's got his mother's heart in him, you can tell that."

Rollins more than met expectations on the court, averaging 16 points a game and making the All-West Coast Conference first team as a senior. And the cap and gown bore testament to his dedication as a student.

After graduation, and when the attempts to catch on in various pro leagues are through? Well, he had a college degree to fall back on.

"What I want to do is get into developing kids, working with at-risk youths," he said. "I want to get back into child psychology, which was my initial area of study. I want to go back to school for that so I can work with kids who've been through some of the things I've been through. They need to know it might be a little harder at the time, but it's a lot more gratifying in the end if you take the right route and make the right choices."

LoRo Takes the High Road

As a GU player and longtime faculty representative, Ken Anderson watched players come to Gonzaga and plow through their course work for more than two decades. Mostly it's been a succession of "solid kids with solid backgrounds," Anderson said.

But for success stories, for pulling off the academic "upset," few could match Lorenzo Rollins's academic odyssey.

"What Lorenzo accomplished may be the greatest achievement I've seen over the span of maybe 30 years," Anderson said. "Given where he'd been and what he managed to do, it was really impressive."

Why? It's the Zags

Former baseball coach Steve Hertz read something in the paper that signaled a permanent change around GU. Hot prospect Cory Violette had just signed to play with the Zags.

"In the article in the paper, he was asked why he signed here," Hertz said. "I'll never forget, he said, 'Because it's Gonzaga.' That was the reason, pure and simple, because it was Gonzaga."

He didn't say "Gonzales," he didn't have to spell it out. He came because it was Gonzaga.

These days, that's all the explanation that's needed.